HEALING PROMISES

Healing
Promises

*The Essential Guide to the
Sacred Heart of Jesus*

ANNE COSTA

franciscan
media
Cincinnati, Ohio

Nihil Obstat: Rev. Darr F. Schoenhofen
Censor Librorum
Imprimatur: Most Rev. Robert J. Cunningham
Bishop of Syracuse
October 26, 2018

The *nihil obstat* and *imprimatur* are official declarations that a book is free from doctrinal or moral error. No implication is contained therein that those who grant the *nihil obstat* or *imprimatur* agree with the contents, opinions, or statements expressed.

Cover and book design by Mark Sullivan

Library of Congress Cataloging-in-Publication Data
Names: Costa, Anne, author.
Title: Healing promises : the essential guide to the Sacred Heart of Jesus /
    Anne Costa.
Description: Cincinnati : Servant, 2017. | Includes bibliographical
    references.
Identifiers: LCCN 2017007391 | ISBN 9781632530967 (trade paper)
Subjects: LCSH: Sacred Heart, Devotion to. | Spiritual life—Catholic Church.
    | Alacoque, Marguerite Marie, Saint, 1647-1690.
Classification: LCC BX2157 .C68 2017 | DDC 232—dc23
LC record available at https://lccn.loc.gov/2017007391

ISBN 978-1-63253-096-7

Published by Franciscan Media
28 W. Liberty St.
Cincinnati, OH 45202
www.FranciscanMedia.org

♥

Dedicated to Gloria Anson
and her Jack
and
all little souls devoted to
the Sacred Heart of Jesus

♥

"O my Jesus and my Love, take all that I have and all that I am, and possess me to the full extent of Thy good pleasure, since all I have is Thine without reserve. Transform me entirely into Thyself, so that I may no longer be able to separate myself from Thee for a single moment, and that I may no longer act but by the impulse of Thy pure love."[1]

—St. Margaret Mary Alacoque

♥

♥ Contents

Healing Promises: An Essential Guide to the Sacred Heart of Jesus will draw everyone who reads it into a deeper relationship with God, a greater understanding of his love for us, and a desire to want to love him in return. She brings the reader on a journey—a journey of the heart. The reason that many do not love Jesus is because they do not know him and the thoughts of his Heart for all generations.

The power of Anne's introduction whets our appetite to want to know more and this book is the *more*!

The signs of our times bid us to read this book, for Anne is sharing with us the answer to the problems of today with the promises of the Sacred Heart. She puts flesh on the promises through the stories of so many who have experienced this devotion in a profoundly personal way.

I have been in this work of promoting love of the Sacred Heart through the Enthronement for forty-three years, across the country and beyond. I feel honored to recommend this book to you, for it presents to us the "remedy for these times." How timely is this book!

Congratulations, Anne. You have done your work well!

—GLORIA ANSON, president of Sacred Heart Apostolate, Inc.,
a global movement for creating a civilization of
love through the Enthronement

Our human hearts were made to love and to be loved, to give and receive love. Every beat of every heart is made possible through a God who *is* love. But do you know that the very heart of God also beats for you? That is what Jesus said to St. Margaret Mary Alacoque, Apostle of the Heart of Jesus, as he revealed his enflamed heart to her: "Behold this Heart which has so loved men as to spare Itself nothing, even to exhausting and consuming Itself, to testify to them Its love."[1]

This revelation is what we have come to know as the Sacred Heart of Jesus. It is one of the most recognizable devotions of our Catholic faith yet one of the least understood. Many Catholics know the image but have yet to experience the depths of the love story behind it. Christ's fidelity to the promises he offers through this devotion is perhaps the best-kept secret of our faith in these times. In particular, the graces that flow from enthronement of the Sacred Heart are being missed by far too many today.

I must admit that when I was first asked to write a book about the Sacred Heart, I panicked. I wondered how anyone could convey the unfathomable richness of the Sacred Heart of Jesus. And at times, it has been like trying to contain the ocean in a thimble!

In addition, when I first started writing this book, I had only recently been introduced to the devotion and the "world" of Jesus's heart. I was a true beginner, just as you might be right now. But as the project unfolded, it became very clear that this was not my story but his. He is on a quest to reveal his heart for all eternity, and this book is another chapter in that ageless love story.

I can say, without a doubt, that coming to know the Sacred Heart of Jesus has changed my life. Once I was drawn in and filled with a longing to know and love Jesus more and more, another ardent desire occupied my heart—to share this Heart with others.

Others who have embraced this devotion have found that the Sacred Heart of Jesus is a secure refuge and a source of true peace in the midst of the pressures and chaos of modern life. As one woman remarked, "His heart is our hope!" And never have we needed that hope more than we do right now.

In a world where people "look for love in all the wrong places"— settling for second-rate substitutes that can result in addictions, family strife, depression, and suicide—Jesus shows us a way. He is the answer to all our questions, no matter what our age or state of life. He offers solace to those aching for relief. He offers truth to young people who are searching for deeper meaning and security. He restores the dignity and moral center of those who are looking for life and see only death. To each of these weary souls, Jesus says: "Come to me, all you that are weary and are carrying heavy burdens and I will give you rest…learn from me; for I am gentle and humble in heart, and you will find rest for your souls" (Matthew 11:28–29).

Jesus also cries out, "Let anyone who is thirsty come to me, and let the one who believes in me drink. As the Scripture has said, 'Out of the believer's heart shall flow rivers of living water'" (John 7:37–38).

These living waters that flow from within Jesus come straight from his pierced and Sacred Heart. That perfect and passionate heart was punctured by a lance as he hung on the cross for our sins. It was at that moment that Love won out. "The Church was born from the wounded heart of the Redeemer."[2] For all time, Jesus empties himself in love for you and for me, at the same time longing and thirsting for some small return. Our devotion to his Sacred Heart is that return.

There are many ways to express devotion to the Sacred Heart. In this book you will learn about them, about the history of this devotion, and about the relevance of the Sacred Heart for our lives today. You will hear from saints, popes, and ordinary people like you and me who have been touched by the Heart of Jesus. Many have shared their stories with me, and I am privileged to share them with you here.

In an effort to preserve the privacy of those who have shared, some names and identifying facts have been changed (without compromising the heart of the message). Each story highlights some aspect of the graces and blessings that flow from a devotion to the Sacred Heart. As one priest said, "It's so simple!" Yet it is so profound to fall in love with the heart of Jesus!

The first part of the book lays out the history and foundation of the Sacred Heart devotion as we know it today. Our encounter with Jesus's heart, as it is revealed in Scripture, provides a foundation for the rest of the book. The second part explores various aspects of the devotion—prayer, the Eucharist, feast days, and more. We will also look at the relationship between the devotion to the Sacred Heart and those of Divine Mercy and the Immaculate Heart of Mary.

Part III covers the twelve promises that Jesus gave to St. Margaret Mary Alacoque in private revelation. I pray that you will come to know and trust in these promises and experience the graces Jesus extends so faithfully and generously to those who are devoted to his Sacred Heart. For when we consecrate ourselves to his heart, we enter into a whole new way of life.

Throughout this book there are ♥ Heart Notes ♥ to encourage further reflection and practical ways to bring the Sacred Heart devotion to your life.

Finally, I look forward to sharing with you one of the Sacred Heart devotions that has come to mean so much to me, the Enthronement of the Sacred Heart. In appendix two, you will find a sample enthronement ceremony associated with the ninth promise of the Sacred

Heart, to "bless those places wherein the image of my Sacred Heart shall be exposed and honored."

Additional appendices include prayers associated with the Sacred Heart devotion, as well as prayers for special circumstances. I have also included a list of organizations and apostolates that are affiliated with or promote devotion to the Sacred Heart. A recommended reading list will aid your further study in the school of Jesus's heart.

* * *

There has never been a time when we have needed his love more than we do right now. Families are hurting; people are lonely and confused; as the world can be a very scary place sometimes. Many are on a desperate search but they don't know what they are searching for. Yet, just when we think we have reached our end, the story of his Heart begins anew. It is a story of hope, healing, and love.

You are *not* alone and there *is* a remedy. Together we will journey to the center of his Heart where his promises are real and his message will always be: *You are loved* and *help is on the way!*

In the service of his precious heart,
Anne Costa

Part One

His
Heart
Revealed

Chapter One

The Story of His Heart

The adorable Heart of Jesus wills to establish its reign of
love in every heart, so as to overthrow that of Satan. It
seems to me that He so greatly desires this that He promises great rewards to those who, with good will and in good
earnest, devote themselves to it, according to the means
and to the light He grants them.[1]

—St. Margaret Mary

Do you remember your first awareness or experience of feeling
loved? Maybe you were a child, looking into your mother's eyes.
Or perhaps you were a young adult, completely enraptured by the
warmth of someone's smile. Maybe there was a teacher who commu-
nicated love, or a babysitter who made you feel special, or a sister who
cared for you. Or perhaps you are someone who is still searching for
love.

Even if you have never felt loved or struggled to love, *being* loved is
an ever-present reality and a never-to-be broken promise that flows
directly from the heart of God. *You are loved*, and as St. Augustine
said, "God loves each one of us as if there were only one of us to
love."[2] Think about that! You are loved exclusively and completely by
God. You don't have to compete for or earn God's love or be anybody
different from who you are, because God is in love with *you*. His
Word is plain: "I have loved you with an everlasting love, therefore I
have continued my faithfulness to you" (Jeremiah 31:3).

Through the Sacred Heart of Jesus, we encounter this faithful love of God. Through our devotion to the Sacred Heart, we experience that love in a whole new way. And through the breath of his Holy Spirit, we are inspired to share it with others. In short, devotion to the Sacred Heart is our return for the unfailing love of God. As author James Kubicki clarifies, "Sacred Heart devotion isn't our devotion... It's God's devotion to us...because God loved us first [1 John 4:19]."[3]

His Heart in Scripture

The first mention of an encounter with the heart of Jesus in Scripture is at the visitation. It was then that, tucked away in the womb of Mary, the newly beating heart of Jesus was recognized by his cousin John the Baptist, who leapt for joy in his own mother's womb. A human heart starts beating at eighteen days after conception, and it would have taken Mary about that amount of time to travel to Elizabeth's house after the annunciation. The reality of Jesus's heart was made known at the earliest possible moment by the very one who would announce the Good News of his coming some thirty years later with the words, "Repent, for the kingdom of heaven has come near!" (Matthew 3:2).

The incredible mystery of the Incarnation is that God willed that a human heart should contain his divine love as a way to be near us and draw us into himself. As we contemplate the beautiful devotion of his heart, we plunge into the depths of the unfathomable love that God has for each one of us. The revelation of God's heart may be seen in the entire life, ministry, and death of Jesus and in the role that the Blessed Mother plays. From the very beginning, their two hearts have been entwined.

Jesus revealed his heart in his encounters with the poor, the rich, the sick, the lame, and the sinner. He reached out to the Samaritan woman at the well, one whom others shunned (see John 4). He had "compassion on the crowd" who had been with him for three days and needed food, which he then provided (Matthew 15:32–38). He wept at the tomb of Lazarus before raising him from the dead (John 11).

Then we come to the Last Supper, where Jesus shows his disciples the full nature of his heart and the depth of his love. At this first Holy Sacrifice of the Mass and every one since, Jesus pours out his heart in the Eucharistic banquet. Father Francis Larkin, who has promoted devotion to the Sacred Heart in our times, gives us a beautiful point to ponder:

> When you receive Jesus in Communion, like St. John, you can rest your head on His Heart.... Each time you participate in the Holy Sacrifice of the Mass, Jesus, from His ever open Heart, pours into your heart—provided it is open and receptive—His Holy Spirit, the spirit of understanding, of wisdom, knowledge and especially love. [4]

St. John, the disciple whom Jesus loved, leaned upon the breast of Jesus, close enough to sense the beating of the Savior's heart. St. Augustine wrote that in these tender moments of closeness, St. John received "Divine Wisdom and the sublime secrets from the innermost depth of Our Lord's Heart."[5] St. Bede the Venerable stated, "Because in Jesus' breast are hidden all the treasures of wisdom and knowledge, it was fitting that the one who leaned upon his breast was the one to whom he had granted a larger gift of unique wisdom and knowledge than to the rest."[6]

St. John went on to accompany the Blessed Mother at the foot of the cross, and there Christ gave him the responsibility of caring for her. John was filled with the Holy Spirit at Pentecost, preached with Peter, and wrote his Gospel and letters, becoming known as the apostle of love. He instructs us to this day: "In this is love, not that we loved God but that he loved us and sent his Son to be the expiation for our sins" (1 John 4:10).

The early Church embraced "the image of John reclining on Jesus' breast as a spiritual symbol of the Church itself. As John drew near to the Heart of Jesus, so the Church is called to draw near to her Lord. There the Church will learn the secrets of his heart. There the Church will find wisdom and courage."[7]

His Heart for the Church

St. Gertrude of Saxony (1256–1302) was a mystic devoted to our Lord's Sacred Heart. The Lord revealed his heart to her many times, in different forms. In these visions, the Lord showed his heart as a "treasury in which all riches are contained and again as a harp which is played upon by the Holy Spirit. His heart was also represented as a fountain from which waters flow to refresh the souls in purgatory, strengthen those on earth and fill the blessed in heaven with incomparable delights."[8]

St. John, the beloved disciple and evangelist, appeared to St. Gertrude, and she took the opportunity to ask him about the tender moments he shared with Jesus at the Last Supper. She was curious as to why he had not written about that encounter to further instruct the faithful. He replied:

> My mission was to write for the Church, still in its infancy.... As for the language of these blessed beats of the Heart of Jesus, it is reserved for the last ages, when the world, grown old and become cold in the love of God, will need to be warmed again by the revelation of these mysteries.[9]

Many believe that we are in these "last ages." The revitalized interest in devotion to the Sacred Heart could be an indication of that. Instead of becoming frightened at the state the world is in, let us be encouraged and comforted. The Sacred Heart is both our shelter and our strength.

This heart was pierced for us on the cross.

> When they came to Jesus and saw that he was already dead, they did not break his legs. Instead, one of the soldiers pierced his side with a spear, and at once blood and water came out. (He who saw this has testified so that you also may believe. His testimony is true, and he knows that he tells the truth.) These things occurred so that the scripture might be fulfilled, "None of his bones shall be broken." And again another passage of scripture says: "They will look on the one whom they have pierced." (John 19: 33–37)

It seems that as soon as the blood and water gushed out, *truth* took over. John testifies to it repeatedly in this passage. Some reflections from the early Church fathers highlight the importance of this piercing as the beginning of our Catholic faith and our Church.

> "There flowed from his side water and blood." Beloved, do not pass over this mystery without thought; it has yet another hidden meaning, which I will explain to you. I said that water and blood symbolized baptism and the holy Eucharist. From these two sacraments the Church is born: from baptism, "the cleansing water that gives rebirth and renewal through the Holy Spirit," and from the holy Eucharist. Since the symbols of baptism and the Eucharist flowed from his side, it was from his side that Christ fashioned the Church, as he had fashioned Eve from the side of Adam….[10]

St. Augustine wrote of the wound: "There it was that the gate of life was opened, from there the sacraments of the Church flow; without these one does not enter true life."[11]

Jesus spoke about this wonderful mystery when he conversed with the Samaritan woman at the well. "Everyone who drinks of this water will be thirsty again, but those who drink of the water that I will give them will never be thirsty. The water that I will give will become in them a spring of water gushing up to eternal life" (John 4:13–14).

Even after he rose from the dead, Jesus bore his wounds as a testament of his love for us. The intimate encounter between St. Thomas and Jesus is a standing invitation for all of us. Thomas proclaimed, "My Lord and my God!" When we have times of fear or struggle or doubt, Jesus desires to come to our aid, calm our fears, and show us the way to belief and trust in him.

"The wound of the body also reveals the spiritual wound," St. Bonaventure stated. "Let us look to the visible wound as the invisible wound of love!"[12]

♥ *Heart Note* ♥

Take some time to enter into a Gospel scene that tugs on your heart. Here are some to consider:

The Visitation (Luke 1:39–45)

The Woman at the Well (John 4:1–42)

The Last Supper (Matthew 26:17–30 or Luke 22:7–38)

Jesus's Meeting with Thomas (John 20:24–29)

As you read, place yourself as a central character in the account, and let Jesus speak to you. Through your prayer, reflection, and dialogue, Jesus may reveal a part of his heart that you have never known. He may even reveal a part of your own heart of which you are not aware.

Open yourself to a true "heart to heart" conversation, in which you can initiate or increase your knowledge of and devotion to the heart of Jesus. Even if you feel that nothing is happening, something truly is. Remember, all that is visible and invisible is revealed through his heart.

HIS HEART IN THE EUCHARIST

Father John Croiset, the Jesuit priest who gave spiritual direction to St. Margaret Mary, stated:

> The devotion to the Blessed Eucharist and the devotion to the Sacred Heart are not only two sister devotions, in reality they are only one and the same devotion. They complete each other and develop each other; they blend so perfectly together that one cannot go on without the other and their union is absolute.[13]

Fr. Larkin adds:

> The Sacred Heart is the living symbol of the love that led Jesus to institute the Eucharist.... Without devotion to the Eucharist, there isn't any true devotion to the Sacred Heart.... In fact, we can truthfully say that the Eucharist *contains* the Heart of Jesus. His heart is not a picture, or a statue, but a living reality, beating out of love for us in the Blessed Sacrament.[14]

This profound reality was expressed by St. John Chrysostom: "It is to this one source that all the Christian mysteries trace back their origin. And so when you apply your lips to this awesome cup, do it as though you drank that precious blood from the open side of Christ himself."[15]

Jesus understands our human hearts. To help us in our belief, he has permitted Eucharistic miracles throughout the Christian era, many of which are officially approved by the Church. We are not obliged to believe in them, because they come under the category of private revelation. But they exist to encourage a deeper understanding and love for the Eucharist.

In the case of one Eucharistic miracle, modern science has been able to confirm the reality of the presence of the heart of Jesus. The Eucharistic miracle of Lanciano, Italy, occurred in 750 at the Church of St. Francis. A priest celebrating Mass was not sure he believed in the True Presence. Then, at the moment of Consecration, the Host turned to visible flesh, and the wine turned to visible blood. This was in a church full of witnesses.

Today, the flesh is still visible, and the blood has coagulated into five unequal parts, which together weigh the same as each one does separately.

Extensive scientific examination (over five hundred studies) of the two species has revealed some remarkable results:

- The flesh is real flesh consistent with the muscular tissue of a human heart, specifically the left ventricle.
- The blood is human blood of the AB type, a relatively rare type that is also found on the Shroud of Turin and is most characteristic of people of Middle Eastern descent.
- No embalming fluids or preservative agents have been detected in the samples.
- The tests also revealed that the samples of flesh are fresh and *living* tissue, like those of a person alive today.[16]

The awesomeness of the Eucharistic heart is a great mystery, requiring God's grace and the gift of faith, both of which we receive in baptism. The devotion to the Sacred Heart holds the promise of an enkindled joy and awareness of this loving sacrifice that he has made for us and that is re-presented at every Mass. Let us give thanks whenever we receive him.

Carol, who has been spiritually drawn to the Sacred Heart since she was a teenager, speaks of the awesome reality of holding Jesus's heart in her hand when she goes to Communion. She explains how this translates to her daily life:

> The disciples on the road to Emmaus [are an example for us]: After they recognize Jesus in the breaking of the bread, and he vanishes, they exclaim, "Were not our hearts burning with love?" [see Luke 24:32]. You can almost see them scratching their foreheads. I have this line printed in big letters over the door where I go out every morning. I never want to go to bed at night without being able to answer the question with a resounding *yes*! Yes, my heart was burning with love!

♥ *Heart Note* ♥

Can you remember a time when you regarded, held, or consumed Jesus in the Eucharist as the fragile, precious, and priceless treasure that he is? Have you burned with love in his presence? Contemplate these words of Jesus:

> Very truly I tell you, unless you eat the flesh of the Son of Man and drink his blood, you have no life in you. Those who eat my flesh and drink my blood have eternal life, and I will raise them up on the last day; for my flesh is true food, and my blood is true drink. Those who eat my flesh and drink my blood abide in me, and I in them (John 6:53–56).

WHAT DOES THIS MEAN FOR US?

These reflections point to the fact that the foundation—of what we believe, who we are, and how we are loved and redeemed by our

God—is the Sacred Heart of Jesus. Blood and water continue to flow from his wounded heart, giving us the inspiration of the Holy Spirit and the lifeblood and mercy for our souls through the sacraments of the Church, particularly the Eucharist.

Jesus does not wish his heart to be a mystery to us. Rather his heart is an open door; he wears it on his sleeve for us, so to speak. Jesus makes his heart completely available to us. He is meek, he is humble, and he makes himself vulnerable, as he is consumed by love for us and concern for our eternal destiny.

In turn, we are invited to offer our devotion, to have our hearts "burn within us," to offer consolation to Jesus and make reparation for all of our offenses and those of the whole world. He wants us to unite ourselves completely with the flow of love and mercy that pours forth from his heart.

♥ Heart Note ♥

Jesus wants to reveal his heart to us in many ways. What has he shown you about his heart thus far? What more do you want to know?

We can entrust our hearts to Jesus with confidence. After his resurrection and before his ascension, he repeatedly offered his peace. He assured his friends then, and his message remains the same for us today: "Do not let your hearts be troubled" (John 14:1).

Sacred Heart of Jesus, be our peace and safe haven of rest!

Chapter Two

St. Margaret Mary: Apostle of His Heart

Cast yourself often…into His divine Heart and abandon
yourself to all His designs upon you.[1]

—St. Margaret Mary

Our modern-day devotion to the Sacred Heart comes from
a series of very special encounters that Jesus had with a humble
Visitation nun turned saint named Margaret Mary Alacoque. Jesus
called her "the Beloved Disciple of My Heart," and she called him
her "Sovereign Master." She was the chosen instrument that the Lord
used to reveal his heart to us. In a letter, she explained, "If only you
knew how much I feel drawn to love the Sacred Heart of Our Lord
Jesus Christ! It seems to me life has been given me only for that."[2]

Her Early Years

Margaret Mary Alacoque was born on July 22, 1647, in a small town
in Burgundy, France. She was the fifth of seven children born to
Claude Alacoque and Philiberte Lamyn, who were known for their
virtue and piety. From a very young age, Margaret Mary displayed
extraordinary devotion to the Blessed Sacrament and an understanding of the mysteries of God that was well beyond her years. She
is said to have dedicated herself to the Lord at the age of four with
this prayer: "Oh, my Lord, I consecrate to you my purity, and I make

a vow of perpetual chastity," even though she "later confessed that she did not know the meaning of the words *vow* and *chastity!*"[3]

When Margaret Mary was eight years old, her father died of pneumonia, and the comfort and stability that she had always known ended. Her family had been quite well-to-do. Now it was determined that Margaret should go to school elsewhere. She was sent to a convent and was taught by the Urbanist nuns. She loved the convent life, but her time there was short. Within two years, Margaret Mary contracted a rheumatic affliction that kept her ill, weak, and bedridden for the next four years.

Margaret was sent home, where much had changed, and not for the better. Her father's relatives had moved in and were now running the household. Margaret Mary and her mother were treated very poorly and even ignored. During this time, Margaret Mary drew near to the Blessed Mother and made a vow to her, much like the one she had made to her Son so many years earlier. She told the Blessed Mother that if she would assist in her healing, she would become one of her daughters. With that offering, Margaret Mary was instantly restored to perfect health.

By this time, Margaret Mary and her mother were virtually prisoners in their own home. They were not allowed to attend church or even have access to food and other comforts without permission. Added to this suffering was her mother's deteriorating health; she suffered from a bacterial infection of the face. This condition caused great swelling and oozing wounds that were noxious and unsightly. Margaret Mary did not know how to tend to them and feared that her mother would die. She implored her relatives for help, but they were unconcerned. A traveling doctor was finally permitted to enter the home, and he declared that Philiberte would need a miracle to survive.

Margaret Mary turned to the Blessed Sacrament for help and guidance. In the midst of this difficult and sorrowful circumstance, she received the consolation of visions and visitations from Jesus, as she had for most of her life. She did not think these conversations and sightings strange but merely assumed that everyone had mystical experiences of divine help. When she had troubles, she turned to him and was never disappointed.

On the Feast of the Circumcision of Our Lord, Margaret Mary was finally able to get to a church and receive Our Lord. There she asked Jesus to be her mother's physician and remedy and to show her how to nurse Philiberte back to health. She returned home and tended to her mother's open wound the best she could. Within a few days, the wound was healed, and her mother quickly regained her health. Margaret Mary had received the aid of the Blessed Mother and her beloved Lord in her time of great need.

As was the custom in her day, Margaret Mary offered up her physical and spiritual mortifications out of a deep and pure love for the Lord. From her earliest years, she embraced suffering as a way to be close to Jesus in his passion. She denied herself temporal pleasures and fasted frequently. "From the age of ten or twelve, she usually slept on the ground, passing a part of the night in prayer even in the depth of winter."[4] These mortifications prepared her for the mission that was to come. Later she would say that "no other grace can be compared with that of carrying the cross out of love for our Lord."[5]

When Margaret Mary was seventeen, the ownership of her father's estate was reclaimed by Philiberte, and the difficulties with the relatives subsided. Margaret was coming to the age to be married, and her mother kept steady pressure on her to seek out a suitable husband. This meant that Margaret Mary had to step into a social world of parties, adorning herself in fancy attire and doing what she could to attract attention. All of this was contrary to the virtues that she cultivated in her pursuit of a loving relationship with Jesus. One particular incident caused Margaret grief for her entire life:

> I had indeed committed great crimes, for once during the days
> of Carnival, together with other young girls, I disguised myself
> through vain complacency. This has been to me a cause of bitter
> tears and sorrow during my whole life, together with the fault I
> committed in adorning myself in worldly attire….[6]

Ever mindful of her childhood vow to Jesus, Margaret Mary was in turmoil. She did not want to disappoint her mother, but even greater was her fear of offending her Lord and the Blessed Mother. In fact, the Lord would not let her forget her promise. She wrote in her diary:

> He aimed such burning darts at my heart that they pierced and
> consumed it on all sides; and the pain I felt in consequence
> rendered me quite speechless. I felt myself bound…with cords
> and dragged with such force that I was at last constrained to
> follow Him Who called me.[7]

Entering Religious Life

Finally, the Lord made a way for Margaret Mary to enter religious life. He guided her to the exact place that he wanted her to be. On May 25, 1671, she entered the Visitation monastery at Paray-le-Monial, France. She pronounced her final vows as a sister of the Visitation of the Blessed Mother in November of the next year.

The Visitation nuns are a cloistered community, and their founders are St. Francis de Sales and St. Jane de Chantal. Tradition indicates, "St. Francis de Sales was inspired to found an Order in the Church with the purpose of, among other things, giving honor and praise to the adorable Heart of Jesus Christ. There was no other Order in his day that professed to pay homage to the Divine Heart."[8] Margaret Mary had a particular devotion to St. Francis de Sales. Once, while contemplating his picture, she felt interiorly drawn to him and sensed that he was calling her as his daughter.

Convent life was not always easy for St. Margaret Mary. As a novice, "she found it hard to keep herself in the ordinary ways of the spiritual life. She said: 'No matter how much I tried to practice what I was taught, I found it impossible to follow the method of prayer presented to me.'"[9] This was a mortifying experience for Margaret Mary, because she wanted to please her superiors, not draw attention to herself, and simply fulfill her duties out of love for them and Jesus.

Margaret Mary offered up many sacrifices and self-denials in order to remain in a solitary embrace of the cross with her beloved Savior. One such self-denial is widely reported in accounts of her life. It seems that her entire family had an aversion to cheese. None of the members could consume it without having an attack of nausea. Prior to Margaret Mary's entrance into the novitiate, her family members made arrangements to strike the food from her diet, something that was rarely done in orders of those days but was deemed necessary because of the potential violent physical response.

Unfortunately, the matter was overlooked, and not wanting to appear rude or disobedient, Margaret Mary ate the cheese served, with fervent prayer that she might not suffer the consequences. The Lord allowed her the grace to consume cheese for the next twenty years. He gave her this as a way to grow in virtue, for she never overcame her loathing of it.

Even as Margaret Mary suffered much for the sake of love, she was also showered with consolations. From the time of her profession of vows in 1672, she "experienced the 'actual and continuous' presence of our Lord."[10] This entailed constant conversations of the heart with the Lord and his ongoing visitations.

These graces come under the category of "private revelation," as defined by the Catholic Church. The *Catechism of the Catholic Church* states:

> Throughout the ages, there have been so called "private" revelations, some of which have been recognized by authority of the Church. They do not belong, however, to the deposit of faith. It is not their role to improve or complete Christ's definitive Revelation, but to help live more fully by it in a certain period of history.... (CCC, 67)

The Catholic Church puts forth many tests for authenticity of private revelations. The obedience and sanctity of the person receiving them are taken into primary consideration. Other tests include, but are not limited to, whether the message supports Church teaching and advances the sanctity of the faithful.

The revelations experienced by St. Margaret Mary have passed every test. They can be believed and, in fact, have been incorporated into the liturgy of the Church. We observe the Feast of Corpus Christi within two weeks of Pentecost Sunday and the Solemnity of the Sacred Heart shortly after that. The Solemnity of Our Lord Jesus Christ, King of the Universe, which is commonly called the Feast of Christ the King, is celebrated at the end of the liturgical year. These are devotions that Jesus asked of Margaret Mary, and they have become synonymous with the Catholic way of life.

A Message for the Time

During the time Margaret Mary was experiencing revelations, there were two terrible heresies that threatened the faithful. These organized denials of Church teaching were in direct opposition to the love of God for humanity. They were known as Quietism and Jansenism. According to the *Catholic Encyclopedia*, Quietism declared:

> Man's highest perfection consists in a sort of psychic self-annihilation and a consequent absorption of the soul into the Divine Essence even during the present life. In the state of "quietude" the mind is wholly inactive; it no longer thinks or wills on its own account, but remains passive while God acts within it. Quietism is thus generally speaking a sort of false or exaggerated mysticism, which under the guise of the loftiest spirituality contains erroneous notions which, if consistently followed, would prove fatal to morality.[11]

Quietism is akin to some of the Eastern and New Age philosophies that seem so attractive today. The problem is that it promotes an unattainable (and in fact, undesirable) goal of perfection through *one's own efforts to remain totally passive*. Quietism also denigrates the physical aspects of the self. It turns people away from God, because they perceive him as demanding the impossible.

Jansenism is named after Bishop Cornelius Jansen, a Dutchman who lived in the early seventeenth century. Jansen was heavily influenced by the Calvinists of his day, who were strong proponents of predestination. His writings, which he intended to remain private but which were published after his death, proclaimed that man had no free will and that we could neither accept nor reject God's grace. Almost fifty years after his death, his ideas took hold in France and beyond, permeating every aspect of society and influencing secular and religious culture.

Proponents of the bishop's thought, who became known as Jansenists, embellished and distorted the message. They believed that humans beings were totally corrupted by original sin and that

Holy Communion should only be received once a year, if at all. For the most part, they believed that ordinary Catholics were not worthy of Communion. As a result, people grew fearful of God instead of loving toward him. They tried to keep their distance rather than be close to him.

The harsh and arbitrary nature of God that the heresy put forth, coupled with the presumed hopeless state of human souls, led people into moral despair. Because people were told that they could not receive God's mercy, they gave up trying to love or please God. They turned against him, believing themselves to be condemned and completely outside of God's mercy.

Given the state of the faithful as a result of these heresies, it seems no coincidence that Jesus would "appear on the scene" to set the record straight. Both his heart and that of his Father were being misrepresented, and his beloved were losing hope and turning away. He chose this exact time in human history to reveal his message through his faithful and loving daughter, St. Margaret Mary, who enjoyed a close union with him. Jesus, with great urgency, proclaimed the true nature of his heart and the depth of his love, making it known to the world once again. He shared these words with St. Margaret Mary: "My love reigns in suffering, it triumphs in humility and rejoices in unity."[12]

The First Apparition

There were four specific apparitions that gave the world the beautiful devotion of the Sacred Heart. These all took place in the chapel at Paray-le-Monial, France, where St. Margaret Mary's body lies incorrupt today. The first one occurred during a time of Eucharistic Adoration on December 27, 1673. St. Margaret Mary's own words describe what happened:

I was praying before the Blessed Sacrament when I felt myself wholly penetrated with that Divine Presence, but to such a degree that I lost all thought of myself and the place where I was, and abandoned myself to this divine spirit, yielding up my heart to the power of His love…. He made me repose upon his sacred Breast and disclosed to me the marvels of his love and the inexplicable secrets of His Sacred Heart…. He said:

> My divine heart is so inflamed with love for men, and for you in particular that, being unable any longer to contain within Itself the flames of its burning love, it needs to spread them abroad through you, and manifest Itself to them in order to enrich them with the precious treasures which I make known to you…. I now give you [the name] of the beloved disciple of my Sacred Heart.[13]

Jesus then asked Margaret Mary for her heart. She gave it to him, and he placed it in his own heart for a time, then returned it to her as she heard him say:

> There, my well-beloved, that's a precious proof of my love for you, hiding in your side a little spark from Its hottest flames. That will be your heart from now on—it will burn you up to your very last breath….[14]

Following this apparition, Sr. Margaret Mary was consumed by the fire of love from the Sacred Heart of Jesus and by the mission of making it known to the world. Even so, she wrestled with reporting her visions to her superiors. She trusted in Jesus, believed she was operating in submission to him, and was convinced of the guidance she was receiving from the Holy Spirit. However, her deep and sincere humility made it difficult to comprehend why the Lord would favor her with such a marvelous task.

When she finally confided in her superiors and her spiritual director, they did not accept what she said and even ridiculed her. She was forbidden from following the inspirations of the Holy Spirit. This was a great trial. Jesus repeatedly reminded her that she must be completely obedient to her earthly superiors as a way of increasing the merit of her offerings. Jesus consoled her as he continued to reveal his heart and mission to her.

THE SECOND AND THIRD APPARITIONS

The second apparition took place sometime in late 1673 or early 1674. In this encounter, Jesus focused on humanity's response to his love. St. Margaret Mary described the image of the Sacred Heart and its meaning:

> I saw this Divine Heart as on a throne of flames more brilliant than the sun and as transparent as crystal. It had its adorable wound and was encircled with a crown of thorns which signified the pain our sins caused Him. It was surmounted by a cross which signified that from the very first moment of His Incarnation…the cross was planted in it.[15]

Jesus said to her:

> This hurts me more than everything I suffered in my passion. Even a little love from them in return—and I shall regard all that I have done for them as next to nothing, and look for a way of doing still more. But no, all my eager efforts for their welfare meet with nothing but coldness and dislike. Do me the kindness then—you at least—of making up for all of their ingratitude, as far as you can.[16]

We can clearly see how Jesus's words in this second apparition are for our current times. Many do not believe in his true presence in the

Eucharist, and homes and churches have been stripped of his image. People are living in desperation because they do not know how much Jesus loves them. He is knocking on the doors of our hearts and desiring to reveal his own heart to us, just as he did to Margaret Mary. It is up to us to answer that call and invite him in.

Jesus asks those who love him to make up for the rejection he experiences, to make reparation. We might wonder, "How do we do that?" St. Margaret Mary shared the desire of Jesus's heart as revealed in this second apparition:

> It [His Heart] must be honored under the symbol of this Heart of flesh, whose image He wished to be publicly exposed. He wanted me to carry it on my person, over my heart, that He might imprint His love there…and destroy all inordinate affections. Wherever this sacred image would be exposed for veneration, He would pour forth His graces and blessings.
>
> This devotion was a last effort of His love in which He wished to favor men in these last centuries with this loving redemption in order to withdraw them from the empire of Satan, which is intended to destroy, and put us under the sweet empire of His love. This He would establish in the hearts of all those who embrace this devotion.[17]

In the third apparition, Jesus gave very specific instructions that continue the framework of the Sacred Heart Devotion:

> Don't be afraid. Simply focus your attention on my voice—First of all, you are to receive Me in the Holy Eucharist as often as obedience allows…. You are to receive Communion on the first Friday of each month. Then every Thursday night…you are to get up between eleven o'clock and midnight [as in the Garden of Gethsemane after the Last Supper] to keep me company in humble prayer to my Father.[18]

Sometime after this third apparition, two people were instrumental in discerning the extraordinary things Sr. Margaret Mary was experiencing. First her superior, Mother Marie-Françoise de Saumaise (Mother Saumaise), came to believe in the truth of the visions. Then, as Jesus had promised, a confessor and spiritual director, the Jesuit priest St. Claude de la Colombière, came into her life. This humble priest was canonized by Pope John Paul II on May 31, 1992, and is known still today for his influence and authenticity as a master spiritual director.

Mother Saumaise commanded Sr. Mary Margaret to tell Fr. Claude everything. He in turn directed Margaret to write down all that she had encountered and knew of the Sacred Heart through Jesus. St. Claude became a pivotal figure in promulgating the devotion of the Sacred Heart as we know it today. He skillfully and lovingly guided Margaret Mary. After the fourth apparition, he "collaborated with the revelation by preaching missions, giving retreats of the Sacred Heart, and by making his own consecration to the Sacred Heart."[19]

THE FOURTH OR "GREAT" APPARITION

The apparition that took place in June 1675, during the octave of the Feast of Corpus Christi, is seen as a culmination of the presentation of the devotion. In it, Jesus said,

> Behold this heart which has loved men so much, that it has spared nothing even to exhausting and consuming Itself in order to testify to Its love; and in return I receive from the greater number nothing but ingratitude by reason of their irreverence and sacrileges, and by the coldness and contempt they show me in this Sacrament of Love.[20]

These words truly pierce the heart of anyone who seeks to love Jesus. They express his sorrow and pain because of our sins and lack of reverence and attention. But Jesus gave us a remedy in this devotion, a means to repair the damage of neglect:

> What hurts me the most is that hearts dedicated to my service behave in this way. That is why I am asking you to have the Friday after the octave of Corpus Christi set apart as a special feast in honor of my Heart—a day in which to receive Holy Communion and make a solemn act of reparation for the indignities I have received in the Blessed Sacrament while exposed on the altars of the world. *I promise that I shall open my Heart to all who honor me in this way, and who get others to do the same; they will feel in all its fullness the power of my love.*[21]

Within a year after the fourth apparition, Fr. Colombière was transferred from his post, away from Margaret Mary. Though she attempted to spread the devotion on her own, there was no public embrace of it for the next ten years! During this time, Margaret Mary suffered greatly but continued to receive further instruction from Our Lord. In spite of all opposition, she wrote Colombière that "she would never despair of seeing it established since she had heard Our Savior say: '*My daughter, do not be cast down by so much opposition. I will reign in spite of My enemies and I will accomplish the design for which I have chosen you.*'"[22]

Finally, in 1685, Sr. Margaret Mary was made mistress of novices at the convent. While this position gave her some measure of authority, another occurrence contributed to a break in opposition to the devotion.

Fr. Colombière had died in 1684. At about the time of St. Margaret Mary's appointment, four volumes of the priest's sermons were published posthumously. In those volumes, he made mention of a favored soul whom he knew personally, who had been given a mission to spread devotion to the Sacred Heart. Even in death, Fr. Colombière aided Sr. Margaret Mary in spreading the devotion. He wrote:

> I have understood that God wants me to serve Him by procuring the accomplishment of His desires concerning the devotion that He revealed to a person [Margaret Mary] to whom He communicates himself very intimately.... I have already suggested this devotion to many people in England and I have written to France asking one of my friends to propagate it.... [I]t will be very fruitful there and be very pleasing to God.[23]

Within a year of the sermons' publication, on June 21, 1686, the first Feast of the Sacred Heart was celebrated. A chapel to the Sacred Heart was built in 1688, and permission was granted to celebrate the Feast of the Sacred Heart in 1689. The devotion spread throughout the Visitation monasteries and beyond. Pope Clement XIII officially recognized and approved the devotion in 1765.

St. Margaret Mary spent the rest of her life, just four short years, dedicated to spreading the devotion. She wrote many letters to her then spiritual director, Jesuit Fr. Jean Croiset. At the Lord's request, she engaged Fr. Croiset in writing a book about the devotion entitled *Devotion to the Sacred Heart of Jesus*. "St. Margaret Mary told Fr. Croiset prophetically that it was so much in line with our Lord's will that it would never need revisions," which has proved true to this day.[24] One paragraph sums up the essence of devotion to the Sacred Heart:

> This Sacred Heart contains an inexhaustible treasure of blessings and graces. I doubt whether there is any exercise in the spiritual life as well adapted to raise a soul to highest perfection in a short amount of time and to make one taste the true sweetness one finds in the service of Jesus Christ. Yes, I am certain

that if people knew how pleasing this devotion is to Jesus Christ there would not be a Christian who would not practice it at once.[25]

Sr. Margaret Mary died at Paray-le-Monial on October 17, 1690. When news of her death reached beyond the monastery walls, townspeople remarked, "The saint is dead." She was beatified by Pope Pius IX on September 18, 1864, and canonized by Pope Benedict XV on May 13, 1920. St. Margaret Mary's feast day is October 17. The monastery at Paray-le-Monial, where her body lies incorrupt, is a place of pilgrimage for those interested in or devoted to the Sacred Heart.

Through these apparitions and the life of St. Margaret Mary, let us fall in love with the Heart of Jesus! How could we not want to offer consolation and devote our attention, hearts, and minds toward his heart? When we do, there are many blessing, graces, and "divine" surprises in store for us.

♥ *Heart Note* ♥

Compose your own prayer to the Sacred Heart. Or recite the prayer to St. Margaret Mary, which may be found in the back of this book (page 191).

Sacred Heart of Jesus, grant that we may always love you more and more.

Part Two

The
Devotion

Chapter Three

Consecration and Reparation: The Foundation

"When our Lord inspires us with some good deed,
He also gives the strength to do it."
—St. Margaret Mary[1]

You might be asking yourself, "So what *is* the devotion to the Sacred Heart? How do you practice it?" Essentially, there are two major components that form its foundation: consecration and reparation.

CONSECRATION

Consecration is the act of setting aside for a sacred purpose. Many Catholic mothers and fathers consecrate their children to the Blessed Mother or to Jesus and his Sacred Heart. When we consecrate ourselves to someone, we proclaim an undivided allegiance or loyalty. In turn, we entrust ourselves to that person's care and purpose.

St. Margaret Mary said, "There is no surer means of attaining perfection [or salvation] than to consecrate oneself to the Sacred Heart of Jesus…. [T]he loving Heart of Jesus will not allow any of those consecrated to it to perish."[2] When we consecrate ourselves to the Sacred Heart, we declare that he is our sovereign Lord, Creator, Savior, and King. We also acknowledge that he is our constant friend and the confidant of our heart, and we dedicate ourselves to serving him.

We can consecrate ourselves to the Sacred Heart of Jesus in either a personal or a communal way. An example of an Act of Consecration to Jesus and his Sacred Heart follows. Saying this prayer on a regular basis, even daily, can bring a great sense of peace and strength to our souls.

> Lord Jesus Christ, I consecrate myself today anew and without reserve to your divine Heart. I consecrate to you my body with all its senses, my soul with all its faculties, my entire being. I consecrate to you all my thoughts, words and deeds, all my sufferings and labors, all my hopes, consolations and joys. In particular, I consecrate to you this poor heart of mine, so that it may love only you and may be consumed as a victim in the fire of your love.
>
> I place my trust in you without reserve, and I hope for the remission of my sins through your infinite mercy. I place within your hands all my cares and anxieties. I promise to love you and to honor you till the last moment of my life, and to spread, as much as I can, devotion to your most Sacred Heart.
>
> Do with me what you will, my Jesus. I deserve no other reward except your greater glory and your holy love. Take this offering of myself and give me a place within your divine Heart forever. Amen.[3]

Communal consecration can take place in families, schools, parishes, dioceses, and even nations. For example, many dioceses are consecrated to the Sacred Heart of Jesus through public enthronement ceremonies and proclamations. Families do the same within their homes. Pope Leo XIII consecrated the entire human race to the Sacred Heart of Jesus on June 9, 1899.

Many families and groups have experienced the blessings that flow from consecration to the Sacred Heart of Jesus. One father of three girls explains that since intentionally consecrating himself and his family to the Sacred Heart four years ago, he and his wife are able to "live the Catholic life" in all of its richness and reward. Even through the pain of two miscarriages and the stresses of daily life, the couple has grown in love and closeness. The father attributes this family cohesion to the presence of Jesus in their midst and the consecration they renew on Sunday nights, when they gather together as a family specifically to pray to the Sacred Heart of Jesus. Their consecration to the Sacred Heart has enabled this entire family to live out the words of Pope Francis, echoing the messages of popes St. John Paul II and Benedict XVI: "Today's world stands in great need of witnesses, not so much of teachers but rather of witnesses. It's not so much about speaking, but rather speaking with our whole lives: living consistently, the very consistency of our lives!"[4]

The special graces and promises that can be claimed through consecration are certainly needed by many today. Imagine the confidence, strength, hope, and peace that families, parishes, schools, seminaries, and dioceses can witness to the world. As this man testified, "The best miracle is right in front of us…. And though we may not always know where we are going, we certainly know *who* is going with us!"

REPARATION

Reparation is the other disposition associated with the Sacred Heart devotion. In a spirit of reparation, we seek to make up for our sins and the sins of others by offering acts of sincere love and sacrifice to Jesus, uniting these acts to his sufferings out of a desire to console his wounded heart.

Jesus informed Margaret Mary very directly that he suffers from the ingratitude, indifference, sacrileges, and sins of man. Our acts of reparation are our way to make up for these and to console him, as we would a hurting friend. We act out of devotion and honor for God, our heavenly Father, who has a right to our love, adoration, and praise. Through reparation, we also acknowledge the Lord's suffering and join in it in some small way. It is his life, death, and resurrection that achieved the ultimate reparation: redemption for all of humanity.

You might wonder how our acts of reparation could have any effect on the Heart of Jesus. How do they console him who is now in heaven, where there can be no suffering? Dr. Timothy O'Donnell, in his book *Heart of the Redeemer,* explains it like this:

> Through offering a loving consolation to our Lord in appreciation of His past sufferings, we attempt a return of love for His infinite love which He manifested on the cross…. In seeking to console the Sacred Heart we are not turning to events which no longer have an effect on us. The effects of our Lord's passion possess an eternal value which do not diminish with the passage of time…. Those who console the Sacred Heart of Jesus are returning love for love at their particular time in salvation history.[5]

Devotion to the Sacred Heart leads us ever more deeply into an awareness and reception of God's love for us. Jesus is not asking for grandiose displays of reparation but simple and heartfelt offerings. He specifically indicated to Margaret Mary that he desired a Communion of Reparation and a Holy Hour, either at church or at home, in remembrance of his agony in the Garden of Gethsemane. Other forms of reparation are resisting sin, offering oneself to the will of God, living a life centered on prayer, offering voluntary penances or sacrifices, and patient acceptance of all of life's trials and difficulties.

Making reparation out of love and concern for Jesus not only expands our hearts but also takes into consideration the welfare of the souls of others. Through reparation, we fulfill the commandment to "love one another" (John 15:17). We offer ourselves and our actions to make up for wounds to the heart of Jesus caused by our own indifference, ingratitude, and offenses of our own sins *as well as those of others*. In doing so, we seek repair, reconciliation, and healing for others as well as ourselves.

Jesus asked Margaret Mary an important question and revealed his intention for asking it: "Behold how sinners treat Me... Will you give me your heart and ease My suffering?... [For] I desire that you may serve Me as an instrument to draw hearts to my Love."[6]

Jesus asks the same question of us today. He revealed to Margaret Mary that his heart is like a fortress, a secure place of refuge for poor sinners. His greatest desire is to pour out his mercies and graces for their benefit. Our acts of "offering up" or joining our sufferings to Jesus's own bring us close to his heart and to him. We can use every trial, inconvenience, sorrow, and pain to save souls. This truth not only transforms our relationship with Jesus but brings great meaning to even the most difficult and confusing storms of our lives.

♥ Heart Note ♥

What act of reparation can you offer out of love for Jesus?

Jim had a very difficult time growing up. His alcoholic father was a hard man who seemed to take all his anger and disillusionment with life out on Jim. Jim tried everything he could to please his father, excelling in school and sports. Even after Jim had established himself in a successful career, his father remained critical and distant, and this caused Jim a great deal of anguish.

As his father was nearing the end of his life, Jim found himself filled with regrets and a growing bitterness. He was plagued with the questions, "Why couldn't things be different? Why couldn't my father show me even a little bit of love or approval?" These questions led

Jim away from God. He felt that even God had rejected him. Finally, however, he sought the counsel of a priest.

The priest listened attentively as Jim poured out his life story. Jim admitted that he was angry with God, bitter, and unforgiving toward his father, who was now failing and in need of his assistance. The priest urged Jim to offer up his sufferings, pain, and disappointment for his father's soul. This sounded not only ridiculous but impossible to Jim. He wondered how in the world he could bring himself to do such a thing to benefit the man who had brought him so much pain. But he resolved to do it, and that is when the miracle began.

The first time was the hardest. Jim went to Mass, got down on his knees, and with clenched teeth and a closed heart, offered his sorrow to Jesus for the sake of his father's soul. Week after week, he silently handed over the sadness, bitterness, and continued stress that the relationship with his father caused him. "I'm giving you this, Jesus, for the sake of my father's soul," he would pray. And over the course of months, he noticed not only that prayer came more easily but that he no longer struggled as much with the desperate feelings.

Jim's relationship with his father changed too. He saw his father with "new eyes," the eyes of Christ, and he felt a growing compassion and understanding toward him. True healing transpired between the two men. In the last years of the elder man's life, they became best friends.

Jim's story demonstrates the gift of reparation that can come to all our lives. Jesus asks us to offer up our sufferings not to repair his heart but to repair our own. When we understand that Jesus shares our pain, that he experiences rejection and sorrow, and when we intentionally join our sufferings to his, something very powerful can happen.

Through the devotion to the Sacred Heart, we are invited to enter into a new way of life. We will receive "a new heart and a new spirit" within us. God will remove "the heart of stone and give...a heart of flesh" (Ezekiel 36:26).

What Is Your Heart Condition?

Do you have a heart of stone, a heart of flesh, or some hybrid of the two? Many of us have hearts that are full of mixed motives, hidden hurts, and divided loyalties. Jesus knows all of this and still loves us. Indeed, he has a fierce desire to take up residence in our hearts, where he can teach us of his love.

Jesus's heart lessons unfold through the devotion to the Sacred Heart. There the Lord makes our hearts like his. According to Margaret Mary, he seeks "purity of intention, humility in action and singleness of purpose."[7] This is only possible when we submit to the reign of his heart and embrace his healing promises with faith. We can think of the elements of the devotion as "spiritual surgery" for our hearts, to restore and transform them to their proper state as sanctuaries for his love.

♥ *Heart Note* ♥

In prayer, ask Jesus to give you a report of your "heart condition." Write down five words (or more) to describe your heart. Ponder them, and ask the Lord to take them into his heart for healing, if need be, or as a gift of gratitude for his love. Then place your hand over your heart, and recite this prayer written by my friend Father Amedeo Guida:

Sacred Heart Prayer

O Jesus, meek and humble of heart, make my heart like yours;
O Jesus, meek and humble of heart, strengthen and protect my heart with your Holy Spirit;

O Jesus, meek and humble of heart, teach me your ways;
O Jesus, meek and humble of heart, heal my heart with the love of your Sacred Heart. Amen.[8]

Sacred Heart of Jesus, fill my heart with your goodness and love!

Chapter Four

Prayer: The First Essential

There are a number of activities that bring devotion to the Sacred Heart alive in our hearts and lives. The Lord's healing promises flow through our embrace of these aspects of the devotion. Love, of course, is at the center of all these actions—love for Jesus and a desire to have that love grow in our hearts as we receive more and more of his love for us.

Certainly prayer is the place to start with any devotion but especially with devotion to the Sacred Heart. That is because it is a devotion that centers exclusively on our love relationship with our Lord. And just like any relationship, our relationship with Jesus requires communication to keep it strong and vibrant. Prayer is our ongoing conversation with Jesus.

Knowing God's Heart

Fr. Croiset wrote: "There is nothing to which Jesus Christ has so often solemnly pledged Himself as to hear our prayers; but of all prayers there is none so agreeable to Him as that by which we ask for his love."[1] Father goes on to say that we are sometimes afraid to ask for God's love because of the demands that his love might place on us. But the more we ask for his love, the more grace he gives us to receive it and act upon it.

It could be said that most of the world's problems, large and small, could be solved if we only knew how much we are truly loved by God. That love covers all manner of sin. Knowing God's love convinces us that we are enough, that we do not need to compete with others, because God's love is an unlimited resource for all.

Fear, often defined as "False Evidence Appearing Real," leads us to believe that we are unlovable, that there is some fundamental flaw in us that makes us unacceptable. Thinking we are unworthy of God's love, we seek false substitutes. The truth is that we *are* unworthy, but that doesn't make God love us any less!

There is a very healthy balance that we can find in devotion to the Sacred Heart, a balance between awareness of our sins and the humility to accept them. We run into trouble when we travel in the extremes: that is, acting as though our sins are not sins at all or at least are of no matter to God; or the opposite, focusing entirely on our wretchedness and unworthiness, which is a form of vanity and hidden pride.

Through prayer, we experience closeness with God and the true love of his heart. This love sets us straight, conquers our fears, and completes us. And in turn, as we come to know the greatness of God's love, we begin to look for ways to help others know it too. Our hope to know and receive God's love in all of its fullness and promise of restoration comes through our prayerful dialogue with the Sacred Heart of Jesus.

In prayer, we can never ask too much of God. In fact, Fr. Croiset says, "The reason why we obtain so little from God is that we do not ask enough, and do not ask it with enough vigor and constancy."[2] St. Margaret Mary explains:

> We can tell him all the secrets of our hearts, disclosing our want and misery to Him who alone can remedy them, and saying, "O Friend of my heart, she whom you love is sick. Visit and heal me, for I know well that you cannot love me and yet leave me alone in my distress."[3]

Short prayers, known as aspirations, have always been a part of devotion to the Sacred Heart. They are "sweet sayings" that we whisper to Jesus out of love for him. Some of the most well-known are "Sacred Heart of Jesus, make my heart like yours," and "Sacred Heart of Jesus, I trust in you." Other aspirations that can be quite effective and bring great comfort in times of stress are "Sacred Heart of Jesus, I believe in your love for me," "Most Sacred Heart of Jesus, grant that I may love you more and more," and "Sacred Heart of Jesus, protect my family and have mercy on us."

♥ *Heart Note* ♥

Take some time to talk with Jesus and share your heart with him in prayer. Tell him your fears and the ways in which you feel unlovable. Ask him for healing. Ask him to show you how much he loves you. Jesus loves to answer these kinds of prayers!

PRAYER FOR OTHERS

Praying for the conversion of sinners is associated directly with devotion to the Sacred Heart. As we will see in Part III of this book, many of the promises of Jesus to those who embrace this devotion focus on securing everlasting life for ourselves and our loved ones. When we spend our lives devoted to him here, we couldn't bear to be separated from him through all eternity, and we don't want that fate for anyone else either! The heart of Jesus is a merciful heart. "The Sacred Heart of our loving Jesus wishes to save many souls…. This divine Heart is like a fortress or secure place of refuge for all poor sinners who wish to take shelter in it from the justice of almighty God."[4]

Praying for the holy souls in purgatory is another hallmark of devotion of the Sacred Heart. St. Margaret Mary had a strong devotion to these souls, whom she called her suffering friends and with whom she was in constant communication mystically. She wrote:

> Would that people knew with what eagerness the poor souls in purgatory ask for this new remedy which is so powerful to relieve their sufferings. They call the devotion to the Sacred Heart the "Sovereign Remedy" and ask particularly for Masses of the Sacred Heart of Jesus.[5]

To aid us in our prayer for the souls in purgatory, it's good to remember that the universal Church is divided into three states: the Church Militant, we who are living and still "fighting the good fight" here on earth; the Church Triumphant, the souls who are in heaven, and the Church Penitent, those souls destined for eternal reward but currently in a purifying state. The *Catechism of the Catholic Church* explains:

> When the Lord comes in glory, and all his angels with him, death will be no more and all things will be subject to him. But at the present time some of his disciples are pilgrims on earth. Others have died and are being purified, while still others are in glory, contemplating "in full light, God himself triune and one, exactly as he is." (*CCC*, 954)

For many who have lost loved ones, the practice of offering Masses and saying prayers for the departed can be a great comfort and a way to stay connected spiritually. The veil of death is just that, a veil that obscures our view and experience of those who have passed on. We can still be united with these souls in prayer. We may be physically separated for a time, but we are still the communion of saints. The holy souls in purgatory can't pray for themselves, but they can pray for us. We can ask them to pray for all our affairs.

♥ *Heart Note* ♥

Consider for whose soul you will offer your next Mass. What prayers will you ask of the holy souls in purgatory? Here's a prayer you can offer for them:

Prayer to the Sacred Heart for Those in Purgatory

Most Sacred Heart of Jesus, remembering the promise of the resurrection, I humbly and sincerely offer these prayers and Masses for [mention your intentions here] and all the departed. With joy, I thank You for what we shared in this earthly life. With hope, I pray this offering will help them on their journey to the fullness of life and happiness with you in heaven. Purify them from all that is not holy, so they may dwell in the mystery of your perfect love forever. With blessed anticipation, I look forward to the coming age, when with your grace, I shall be united with them again in paradise.

Say one Our Father, one Hail Mary, and one Glory Be. Then conclude as follows:

> May the souls of the faithful departed, through the mercy of God, rest in peace. Amen.[6]

* * *

Diane brought up her large family of twelve under the watchful eye of the Sacred Heart of Jesus. Just as her mother had encouraged her as a child to "take everything to Jesus," she likewise instructed each of her children to trust in his Heart. As they grew, she felt confident that he would protect them and keep them from harm, and he did. Yet that doesn't mean they didn't struggle and sometimes fall.

As a teenager, her youngest son got into trouble and landed in jail. It was a devastating and scary time for him and for Diane, who clung to the promises of Our Lord and prayed fervently for the conversion of her son. She felt very strongly that this prayer was answered. Even though her son struggled with perpetual sin, he never lost his faith and always relied on Jesus and Mother Mary.

One night, Diane could not get in touch with her son in jail. She could neither visit him nor reach him by phone. So she got down on her knees and prayed, asking Jesus to send his Blessed Mother in her place to be with her son. She mentally tucked the prayer into the wound in the Sacred Heart of Jesus and went to sleep.

The next morning, Diane's son called and excitedly explained to his mother, "I had the strongest sense that Our Lady came right into my cell and wrapped her arms around me!" Diane was overjoyed in the realization that her prayer was heard and answered. She knew in her heart that her son's troubles would end. She was right. Today he is a faith-filled father of five.

Sacred Heart of Jesus, we place our trust in you!

Chapter Five

The Eucharist

St. Claude de la Colombière, St. Margaret Mary's spiritual director, reflected:

> God is more honored by a single Mass than He could be by all actions of angels and men together, however fervent and heroic they might be…. If we only knew the treasure we hold in our hands…. [I]n the adorable Sacrifice they can find all things: graces, riches, spiritual and temporal, favors for body and mind for life and eternity.[1]

As stated in the first chapter, the devotion to the Sacred Heart is a Eucharistic devotion because Jesus is present—Body, Blood, Soul, and Divinity—in the Eucharist. This includes his Sacred Heart. We seek union and communion with him because, as with anyone whom we love, we desire to be as close as possible, as often as possible.

At Holy Mass, we enter into the heart of Jesus, who is offered as the perfect sacrifice to the Father through the Holy Spirit. Thus the Mass is alive and eternal; it is the truest and highest means of uniting ourselves with Jesus. Embracing the Sacred Heart devotion opens the door to a revived or enkindled awe and reverence when receiving Jesus in the Eucharist. Remembering that indifference offends him, we are led to receive him with the deepest respect and openness to his love. The intimacy of the act comes to life in our hearts. Communion draws us into the depths of his heart.

FREQUENT COMMUNIONS

Pope Emeritus Benedict XVI said of the Eucharist, "God no longer simply stands before us, as the One who is totally Other. He is within us, and we are in him."[2] And it is through frequent Communions that we receive the grace and strength to carry him and his love out into the world, to others. While many of the activities of the devotion to the Sacred Heart are personal ones that we engage in alone or within the family unit, it is our Lord's desire that the fruit of the devotion burst forth into all of our relationships and encounters. The reign of his heart cannot be accomplished without our sharing the love that he showers upon us in the Eucharist and through his Sacred Heart.

There were times in the historical tradition of the Church when frequent Communions were discouraged or prohibited. This was actually the case during the times of St. Margaret Mary and St. Claude. When someone suggested to St. Claude that he shouldn't encourage frequent Communions, even adding that the devil was making him do it, he responded,

> Do not come to me with such arguments. I began to amend my life by frequenting Holy Communion after having tried every other way and failed…. My daily Mass and Communion is my only hope and resource. Jesus can do very little if he cannot uphold me from day to day.[3]

Of course, Jesus wants us to come to him in Communion out of love and the desire to receive him, not by mere duty or obligation. Sometimes our state in life and daily responsibilities make it difficult to get to Mass on a daily basis or as often as we might like. For these circumstances, the Church offers and recognizes Spiritual Communions.

An Act of Spiritual Communion is an intentional desire to receive

Jesus in Holy Communion even though we are not physically able to do so. St. Alphonsus Liguori instructed, "Spiritual Communion produces effects in our souls similar to Sacramental Communion, according to the dispositions of our hearts."[4] He wrote the prayer that accompanies an act of Spiritual Communion:

> My Jesus, I believe that You are present in the Most Holy Sacrament, I love You above all things, and I desire to receive you into my soul. Since I cannot at this moment receive You sacramentally, come at least spiritually into my heart. (Pause)
>
> Dear Jesus, I embrace You as if You were already here, and I unite myself wholly to You. Never permit me to be separated from you. Amen.[5]

Making a Spiritual Communion is an act of love. By uniting ourselves with Jesus spiritually, we essentially make a "heart-to-heart" connection with his Sacred Heart. There are no limits to the number of Spiritual Communions we can make in a day. Each time we make one, we bring great joy and consolation to Jesus.

♥ *Heart Note* ♥

Look for a prayer card that contains the Spiritual Communion Prayer, or write the prayer on an index card and laminate it. Place it in an easily accessible place, where you can be reminded to make Acts of Spiritual Communion throughout the day.

FIRST FRIDAYS

Jesus was specific with his instructions regarding this part of the devotion. His request is that the faithful go to confession or attend Mass and worthily receive Communion, and offer prayers for the intention of the Holy Father on the First Friday of every month for nine consecutive months. Jesus made great promises to those who faithfully carry out this part of the devotion. He said he would grant them the grace of final repentance: They will not die under his displeasure nor without receiving the sacraments, and they will be assured of refuge at their final hour.

The Church grants a plenary indulgence to the faithful who attend Mass and receive Communion in honor of the Sacred Heart on the first Friday of every month. A plenary indulgence "is the remission before God of [all] the temporal punishment due to sins whose guilt has already been forgiven" (*CCC*, 1471). An indulgence can be applied to oneself or to a deceased person. It cannot be applied to any other living person, and only one indulgence can be gained per day. The prescribed conditions also include being in a state of grace, with complete detachment from sins, even venial ones.

We can sometimes take what Jesus says so literally that we miss the spirit and intention of his message. If there have been any criticisms or misunderstanding of the devotion to the Sacred Heart, they usually revolve around this aspect. What may have happened historically is that people carried out Jesus's requests ritualistically or superstitiously, in order to "get to heaven," without expressing the deep love or experiencing the healing that was intended to accompany the actions.

Dr. Timothy O'Donnell explains that the promise surrounding the practice of First Fridays "was made to the person who completely surrenders himself in a deep and unconditional act of faith. It is a beautiful expression of the Lord's desire to share Himself with us in His sacrament of love."[6] As with any devotion, the outward observance is never as important as the inward experience. Observing First Fridays is an invitation to offer an act of faith and love to Jesus, pure and simple.

In our modern times, making time for First Friday devotions can be a sacrifice, but it is one worth making. What's most important is not that we legalistically fulfill its obligations but that we approach it with sincere and simple love in our hearts. We make a special effort, and God looks at our hearts and knows our motives and intentions. We do the best we can, and he is pleased with us.

We could say that First Friday is a devotion of consolation and presence. We show our love to Jesus by "making a habit" of drawing near to his heart, both interiorly and in the world, through inward and outward gestures of being "present" to him. As Fr. Larkin remarked, "The Holy Sacrifice of the Mass is without doubt the best means of showing our love for the Sacred Heart, as it is our Lord's best way of proving His love for us."[7]

THE APOSTLESHIP OF PRAYER

One resource that we have today to help us complete the First Friday devotion is the Apostleship of Prayer. It is a worldwide prayer network that makes known the pope's monthly prayer intentions. This helps Catholics satisfy the request that Jesus made, that we pray for the Holy Father's intention on First Fridays.

The mission of the Apostleship of Prayer is to encourage Christians to make a daily offering of themselves to the Lord for the coming of God's Kingdom and for the Holy Father's monthly intentions. This habit of prayer encourages a Eucharistic spirituality of solidarity with the Body of Christ and loving service to others. Nourishing this spiritual program is the love of the Sacred Heart of Jesus.[8]

In the second apparition, Margaret Mary related Jesus's desire that his heart be honored and that she carry on her person, over her heart, an image of his love. This inspired the Sacred Heart Badge, a sacramental produced and distributed by the Apostleship of Prayer and others. The badge is typically double-sided, with a picture of the Sacred Heart on one side and an image of Our Lord on the other. There are also two short aspirations: "Sacred Heart of Jesus, Thy Kingdom Come" and "Cease, the Heart of Jesus is with me."

The badge is an emblem of love, not associated with any protective powers on its own. Wearing it is much the same as wearing a crucifix around one's neck. As with any sacramental, it is the faith and the devotion of the person that matters. The *Catechism of the Catholic Church* tells us, "Sacramentals are sacred signs instituted by the Church. They prepare men to receive the fruit of the sacraments and sanctify different circumstances of life" (*CCC*, 1677).

We live in a very visual world, with a tremendous amount of information and stimulation coming to us from every angle. We need reminders and mementos upon which to focus in order to combat these myriad distractions. Any means by which we can relate to Jesus, even for a moment, will help us orient our hearts toward him. The Sacred Heart badge is one way of doing it.

I have my badge attached to my keychain. It's a gentle reminder that my heart belongs to Jesus and that he is with me always.

Thirty-Three Visits

Those who cannot carry out the First Friday aspect of the devotion may want to consider a lesser known one, that of the thirty-three visits to the Lord on the cross. It is another way that our Lord gave St. Margaret Mary to bring honor and joy to his heart. "[Jesus] told me lovingly that He desired me every Friday to adore Him thirty-three times upon the cross, the throne of his mercy…in the Dispositions of the Blessed Virgin Mary during His Passion."[9]

Already we know that Friday is a day we set aside to contemplate the passion of Jesus. Margaret Mary was instructed to offer her acts of adoration to the Father especially for those with hardened hearts who resist God's grace. Here are further instructions for this devotion:

> These thirty-three acts of adoration of our Lord on the cross may be made anywhere on Fridays, and even while attending to one's ordinary work. They require no special attitude, formula or vocal prayer. A simple look of love and contrition coming from the depth of our hearts and sent up to our crucified Lord is sufficient to express our adoration, and our gratitude to Him.[10]

There is a temptation, especially in our Western culture, to think that bigger is better, that the more splash we make, the greater will be our significance. Jesus shows us something different. He seeks the sweet nothings of a soul that recollects itself quietly and in a very hidden way, as does his mother. So when entering into this devotion, there is no need to scrupulously count the number of times we stop to reflect upon Jesus. Soon enough, it will become a habit of the heart that brings consolation to us and to him.

Weekly Holy Hours

Jesus directly asked Margaret Mary to spend one hour with him on Thursdays (specifically, between 11:00 PM and midnight) to console his heart, just as he had asked the disciples Peter, James, and John to do in the Garden of Gethsemane on Holy Thursday night. Many families devoted to the Sacred Heart keep this Holy Hour together before the image on a weekly basis or monthly, on the Thursday before First Friday. They dedicate this time to offering prayers to Jesus, saying the rosary together, or reading Scripture or writings about the Sacred Heart.

Pope Emeritus Benedict XVI stated, "The very core of Christianity is expressed in the heart of Jesus."[11] So when we set aside a dedicated hour to contemplate the heart of Jesus and his Eucharistic Presence, some very important things happen. Individuals and families experience a new depth of love and self-giving and an increased awareness of God within their souls, all inspired by Jesus.

One mother of three small children, all under the age of eight, remarked, "These Holy Hours are like the glue that holds our family together." She bought her children Sacred Heart coloring books to use while she and her husband prayed. She found that the children looked forward to their "Jesus" time and often were the ones who kept the schedule going!

An apostolate devoted to the keeping of the Holy Hour is known as the Guard of Honor of the Sacred Heart of Jesus. It was formed as an association of the faithful in 1863 and put forth by Sr. Marie of the Sacred Heart Bernaud, who was a Visitation nun like St. Margaret Mary. She lived in a monastery closely connected with the one in Paray-le-Monial, where Margaret Mary lived. The Guard of Honor is now an archconfraternity and has members all around the world. Each chooses one hour of guard a day to console the wounded heart of Jesus, make reparation, and attend to Christ's burning love for us.

As with the thirty-three visits devotion, "It is not necessary to spend the Hour of Guard in prayer, nor in church. At their chosen hour...member[s], without changing any of their usual occupations, place themselves in spirit at the foot of the tabernacle. There they offer to Jesus their thoughts, words, actions and sufferings, and above all their desire to console His divine Heart by their love."[12]

The image of the guard is a "dial" of twelve stars surrounding the Sacred Heart of Jesus, with the words "LIVE+JESUS" above. Each star represents an hour on the clock and is devoted to a specific intention. Around the world, there is perpetual adoration and contemplation of our Lord's Sacred Heart by members. Here is their Prayer of Offering:

Lord Jesus, present in the tabernacle, I offer this hour to You with all my actions, my joys and my sorrows, to glorify Your Heart by this testimony of love and reparation. May this offering benefit my brothers and sisters and make me a more zealous laborer for the accomplishment of Your loving designs for humanity. With You and for them, "I consecrate myself for them, so that they may also be consecrated in truth" (John 17:19). Amen.[13]

Visits to the Blessed Sacrament

Visits to the Blessed Sacrament can sustain us in the midst of our stressful lives. They are a proven means of receiving God's grace and peace and of strengthening our relationship with him. As Fr. Croiset pointed out, friendship requires "frequent visits and conversations… and it is by [visiting the Blessed Sacrament] that we gain and increase in the friendship of Jesus Christ."[14]

Visits to our Lord in the Blessed Sacrament afford us the opportunity to celebrate his continual presence with us and to praise him, bless him, adore him, glorify him, and give him praise for his great glory, as we say in the Gloria at Sunday Mass. It also is a way for us to simply share our hearts and hurts with Jesus, as well as our triumphs and joys.

St. Francis de Sales said, "Of all the devotions, that of adoring Jesus in the Blessed Sacrament is the greatest, after the sacraments, the one dearest to God and the one most helpful to us."[15] Even a few minutes contemplating him can bring joy to our souls. And how the world might be changed if we who love Jesus spent time in his presence on a regular basis!

Perhaps your church is not open during the day, but don't let that stop you. "Search, and you will find" (Matthew 7:7). Many dioceses have perpetual Adoration chapels, which are open twenty-four hours a day, seven days a week. Many parishes have scheduled times of Adoration.[16]

♥ *Heart Note* ♥

Commit yourself to one visit a week with Jesus at a tabernacle near you!

Sacred Heart of Jesus, may you be loved, praised, and adored in all the tabernacles of the world!

Chapter Six

Solemnities and Feasts

There are many celebrations throughout the liturgical year that are related to devotion to the Sacred Heart.

First and foremost is the Solemnity of the Sacred Heart (widely referred to as the "Feast" of the Sacred Heart), which takes place on the Friday following the second Sunday after Pentecost, the Solemnity of the Body and Blood of Christ. Many parishes have special services or public prayers to the Sacred Heart on that day. Families who have had their homes enthroned or those involved in apostolates devoted to enthronements will often gather for a meal, a small celebration, or a presentation on the Sacred Heart. Since 2002, the Solemnity of the Sacred Heart has also been a special day of prayer for the sanctification of priests.

The Solemnity of the Body and Blood of Christ, also known as Corpus Christi, is another important feast related to the Sacred Heart devotion, as it celebrates the real presence of Jesus in the Eucharist. Many churches have reinstated the practice of a public procession following Mass to venerate the Body and Blood.

Another feast that inspires devotion to the Sacred Heart is the Solemnity of Our Lord Jesus Christ, King of the Universe, commonly referred to as the Feast of Christ the King. We celebrate this on the final Sunday of the liturgical year, the Sunday before the beginning of Advent.

Margaret Mary affectionately called Jesus her "Sovereign Master." He was her King, the Lord of her heart. She urged others to "have no reserve with him who wishes to dwell within you…to rule and govern you…. Let us entreat Him to establish His reign in all hearts."[1]

The Feast of Christ the King celebrates the fact that Jesus is King over the whole world. His kingdom is a holy kingdom that preserves and protects the God-given dignity and freedoms of all.

FEASTS OF SACRED HEART SAINTS

Recognizing and celebrating the saints who are associated with the Sacred Heart, particularly on their feast days, is another nice way to live out the devotion. This is an especially effective way to draw in children, as many of the saints have lived adventurous and heroic lives that are sure to inspire. Children and youth can be engaged in learning about the Sacred Heart saints at every age. We can encourage them to ask the saints' intercession and help.

The first saint that comes to mind, of course, is St. Margaret Mary. Her feast day is October 16. On this day, the Church prays, "Pour out on us, we pray, O Lord, the spirit with which you so remarkably endowed St. Margaret Mary, so that we may come to know that love of Christ which surpasses all understanding and be utterly filled with your fullness."[2]

We celebrate the great St. Francis de Sales (1567–1622) on January 24. A Doctor of the Church, he founded the Visitation order, to which St. Margaret Mary Alacoque belonged. He was deeply devoted to the Sacred Heart and wrote the following prayer:

May thy heart dwell always in our hearts!

May thy blood ever flow in the veins of our souls!

O sun of our hearts, thou givest life to all things by the rays of thy goodness!

I will not go until thy heart has strengthened me, O Lord Jesus!

May the heart of Jesus be the king of my heart!

Blessed be God. Amen.[3]

We celebrate St. Lutgarde's (1182–1246) feast on June 16. Blogger Chloe Mooradian tells us that the Sacred Heart beat inside this saint's chest:

> In the 1200s, St. Lutgarde was visited in a vision by Christ Himself. During the vision, Christ offered St. Lutgarde whatever she wished. She requested a simple gift: to understand the Latin language better so that she could worship Christ in a [fuller] way. The grace of learning was given to her, but St. Lutgarde returned to Christ feeling empty and requested a gift exchange of sorts. Christ asked what He could replace the gift with, and St. Lutgarde requested Christ's heart. So Christ reached into Lutgarde's chest, removed her heart and replaced it with His own Sacred Heart.[4]

On August 19, we celebrate the feast of St. John Eudes (1601–1680), who wrote the first book on the two hearts—the Sacred Heart of Jesus and Mary's Immaculate Heart. St. John's lifelong mission was to encourage the faithful in devotion to the hearts of Jesus and Mary among the faithful. He lived at the same time as St. Margaret Mary, but they never met. He established a Feast of the Sacred Heart three years before she did.

The feast day of St. Bernard of Clairvaux (1070–1153) is August 20. St. Bernard wrote and spoke extensively on the love that the Sacred Heart of Jesus has for us. He particularly focused on the holy wounds of Christ. One time he asked Our Lord which was his greatest unrecorded suffering. Our Lord answered:

> I had on My Shoulder, while I bore My Cross on the Way of Sorrows, a grievous Wound, which was more painful than the others and which is not recorded by men. Honor this Wound with thy devotion, and I will grant thee whatsoever thou dost ask through Its virtue and merit....[5]

The feast of St. Gertrude the Great (1256–1302) is November 16. She enjoyed a continual communion with Our Lord, as he shared his divine heart with her many times. He told her, "My Divine Heart, understanding human inconstancy, desires with incredible ardor to be continually invited, either by words or signs, to operate and accomplish in you what you are unable to accomplish yourself."[6] St. Gertrude is known as the Herald to Devotion to the Sacred Heart of Jesus.

On November 19, we celebrate the feast of St. Mechtilde (1240–1298). This dedicated saint, Fr. Croiset tells us,

> [W]as so penetrated with the devotion that all day long she could speak only of this adorable Heart of Jesus and of the singular favors which she received from this devotion. This amiable Savior gave her His Heart as a pledge of His love and to serve her as a place of refuge where she would unceasingly find sweet repose during life, and inexpressible peace and consolation at the hour of death."[7]

Other saints who had a particular devotion to the Sacred Heart are St. Francis of Assisi, St. Teresa of Avila, St. Bonaventure, St. Ignatius, St. Francis Xavier, St. Philip Neri, St. Aloysius Gonzaga, and St. Catherine of Siena. A special visit to the Blessed Sacrament, a prayer of thanksgiving, and attending Mass on these saints' days are a few ways to celebrate the Heart of Jesus and the devotion they lived and worked to establish.

♥ Heart Note ♥

Read a biography of one of the Sacred Heart saints.

THE FEAST OF THE IMMACULATE HEART OF MARY

This feast takes place on the day following the Solemnity of the Sacred Heart. These two days give us an opportunity to contemplate what these two pierced hearts sacrificed for all of us and the love that flows from them to us for all eternity. We'll discuss this more in chapter eight, "Mary, Mother of the Sacred Heart."

In 1942, during World War II, Pope Pius XII dedicated the whole world to the Immaculate Heart of Mary and set a feast day, which was moved in 1969 to its present spot next to the Feast of the Sacred Heart. In 1984, Pope John Paul II renewed the consecration of the world to Mary's Immaculate Heart. Again in the year 2000, he entrusted the world and the new millennium to the Immaculate Heart of Mary.

Pope Francis has continued this papal tradition. On October 13, 2013, the anniversary of Our Lady's appearances at Fatima, Pope Francis announced the consecration of the world to the Immaculate Heart of Mary and asked the Blessed Mother's help: "Guard our lives in your arms. Bless and strengthen every desire for goodness; revive and grow faith; sustain and illuminate hope; arouse and enliven charity; guide all of us on the path to holiness."[8]

The Feast of the Immaculate Heart of Mary reminds us that the love in Mary's heart is a love we seek to imitate. Our generous and selfless mother shares with us many helps and graces. Her only desire is to direct us to her son, so that we might "do whatever he tells us" (see John 2:5). Consecration to Mary's Immaculate Heart can only lead us more swiftly and intimately to the heart of her son.

♥ *Heart Note* ♥

The Prayer of Consecration to the Immaculate Heart of Mary is contained in the Enthronement Ceremony (see appendix two). Is this something you should consider for your home?

Sacred Heart of Jesus, I give myself to you through Mary!

Chapter Seven

Enthronement of the Sacred Heart

Enthronement is a cornerstone of the devotion to the Sacred Heart, as it incorporates many of the promises that Jesus made to St. Margaret Mary, in particular the ninth promise: "I will bless the homes where an image of my heart shall be exposed and honored."

A good explanation of what enthronement means comes from Fr. Larkin:

> The Enthronement of the Sacred Heart means the recognition of Jesus, the God-man who is all loving and merciful, as the King and Friend of the family. It means giving our Lord the first place in our hearts, in our family life. It is like a *"heart-exchange"*—Jesus gives His heart to us and we offer our hearts to Him. Under the influence of his grace, He really brings about a transformation of our hearts, our attitudes—changing indifference into love, apathy into action, fear into trust. We become different persons for we have had a change of heart.[1]

From this definition, we can see that enthronement is a powerful means of transforming our families and fortifying them against the forces of our culture that threaten to tear them apart. It's important to note that enthronement is not the worship or adoration of a picture or body part. At various times in human history, God the Father, Jesus Christ, and the Holy Spirit have made requests of certain individuals to create or fashion images to help God's people. This dates back to the Old Testament, when God instructed Moses to make a seraph and mount it on a pole so that the afflicted Israelites could gaze upon it and be healed (see Numbers 21:8–9).

Some have dismissed the devotion to the Sacred Heart, and enthronement in particular, as merely a superficial, outward act of piety with no corresponding interior spirituality. Such people are missing the intention of Our Lord, his desire to inspire and express the depths of his love. Even apart from deliberate devotion, having the image in a prominent place serves its purpose.

One woman shared that her image of Jesus is on a wall in the kitchen, right next to her phone. Many times she has been caught up in conversation only to glance up at Jesus and be inspired to quickly determine if her conversation would "pass muster" with him. Another woman practically stated that it is a matter of "out of sight, out of mind." The image serves to remind her and her family members that Jesus is *always* with them and that he and his heart are a source of protection, healing, and transformation for them.

Peggy and Steve, who have been involved in the Sacred Heart Apostolate for many years, shared at the World Meeting of Families how the image made a difference. They were having some work done at their home when one of the landscapers knocked on the door to ask a question. As Peggy opened the door, the man's gaze went past her and fixed on an object in the distance. Suddenly, the man fell to his knees and blessed himself, saying a quiet prayer.

Peggy realized that the man saw the image of the Sacred Heart hanging prominently over the mantle in their living room and was moved to pay homage to his loving heart right then and there. This simple act of adoration and the humility that the man showed in the middle of his workday moved Peggy to tears. An act of love, inspired by the image, consoled the heart of Jesus during the course of an ordinary day.

The Apostle of Enthronement to the Sacred Heart

The Enthronement Apostolate received its blessing from Pope St. Pius X on August 24, 1907. This came about through the concerted efforts of Father Mateo Crawley-Boevey (1875–1961), who is known as the Apostle of the Sacred Heart Enthronement.

Fr. Mateo was born in Tingo, Peru, to devout parents of English and Peruvian descent. He was the third of eleven children. From a very young age, he attended daily Mass with his grandfather. Mateo was taught and formed by the Fathers of the Sacred Hearts.

At the age of sixteen, Mateo joined the Congregation of the Sacred Hearts of Jesus and Mary in Valparaiso, Chile. He embraced whole-heartedly the purpose of the community—to spread devotion to the Sacred Heart and the Immaculate Heart of Mary through education, adoration, preaching, and making reparation. His early endeavors to make the heart of Jesus known and loved included establishing a school of law as a part of Sacred Hearts College in Valparaiso.[2]

An apparent tragedy became the impetus for the enthronement movement throughout the world. In 1906, an earthquake destroyed the school of law! All of Fr. Mateo's hopes and efforts seemed to be reduced to a pile of rubble, and he was near despair. However, he prayed in faith to God. Later he stated that, had it not been for the earthquake, he would not have become a "globetrotter" for the Sacred Heart.

One of the few things that was not destroyed by the earthquake was a large oil painting of the Sacred Heart. It was a picture Fr. Mateo cherished. It represented all he had been working toward. The fact that it had been "protected" was a prophetic message that was not lost on Fr. Mateo.

But the immediate needs of the people took precedence, and Fr.

Mateo dedicated himself to relief efforts. The work of rebuilding took a toll on his physical well-being. He was sent to Europe to recover, and there he received his life's commission. While visiting Belgium and France, he formulated his plans to promote love for the Sacred Heart around the world. He shared his thoughts with key people along his journey, and these managed to open doors for him.

When Fr. Mateo went to Rome, a cardinal helped him get an audience with Pope Pius X. The Holy Father told Fr. Mateo directly, "To save the family is to save society. The work you are undertaking is a work of social salvation…. Consecrate your life to it."[3]

Believing that this was a command from Jesus, Fr. Mateo made a pilgrimage to the chapel at Paray-le-Monial, where Jesus had appeared to St. Margaret Mary. There he sought direction and a restoration of his health. His great desire was to fulfill the mission the pope had given him, but he wasn't sure how to do it.

Through fervent prayers of intercession and thanksgiving, Fr. Mateo received not only a spontaneous healing but also the plan for the spiritual work ahead. He said of this momentous event: "I understood what our Lord desired of me…. I resolved upon a plan to conquer the whole world for the love of the Heart of Jesus—home after home, family after family."[4]

Fr. Mateo developed the Sacred Heart enthronement ceremony that is still in use today. He dedicated his life to promoting this devotion throughout the world, aided by several groups dedicated to the cause. Enthronement to the Sacred Heart continues to be a global effort with high levels of interest in Africa, the Philippines, Mexico, South America, and of course, the United States.

Most of these efforts are spearheaded by a small group of people who have, like Fr. Mateo, embraced with great zeal the call to make the Heart of Jesus known, honored, and loved. Many of the stories that are shared in this book come from families and individuals who have enthroned the Sacred Heart image in their homes, places of business, seminaries, and schools.

THE CEREMONY

Appendix one gives instructions on how to prepare for an enthronement of the Sacred Heart in the home. Enthronement is not a complicated process, but it *is* intended to be a solemn event that follows a period of prayer and preparation. A thorough and thoughtful preparation is key to realizing and recognizing the tremendous graces and blessings that flow from an enthronement,

A sample enthronement ceremony and information on how to carry it out is in appendix two. The spirit and activities of the enthronement can be summarized by seven words:

Invitation: We invite Jesus into our lives, homes, and hearts. He is a true gentleman in that he will never come uninvited. He knocks, but we must open the door. "Listen! I am standing at the door, knocking; if you hear my voice and open the door, I will come in to you and eat with you, and you with me" (Revelation 3:20).

Visitation and Preparation: A lay leader, a priest, or a deacon assists the individual or family in preparing for Jesus's coming. This often involves at least one visit, several days or a week before the scheduled enthronement. At this visit, a brief catechesis (teaching) is offered, and prayers (usually including a rosary) are recited. Materials for study, usually in the form of a packet or booklet, are provided.

Also at this visit, a Consecration to the Immaculate Heart of Mary may be conducted (or it may be done following the actual enthronement ceremony). Sometimes a pilgrim statue of Our Lady of Fatima or a similar Marian statue is left in the home, as a reminder of the Blessed Mother's presence and her role in preparing the way for Jesus.

The goal is a sense of joyful anticipation and a deepening understanding of what the impending enthronement will mean for each individual, family, or group.

Installation: A prominent and proper place is chosen for the image. The image should be in a gathering place, indicating that Jesus is the head and Lord of the home or building. A procession within the dwelling to the place of honor is like a pilgrimage within the "domestic church." Each member plays a part.

Consecration: The family (or other group) members consecrate themselves to the Sacred Heart of Jesus. Relatives and friends are invited as witnesses, making this a public proclamation that Jesus is the King of the family. The enthronement ceremony is the outward act of inward conversion of heart.

Celebration: After the ceremony, a celebration is encouraged: a meal or similar social gathering to celebrate the new life of the family in the Sacred Heart of Jesus.

Transformation: No family, group, or individual remains unchanged after an enthronement. God's love transforms. It heals and offers help and consolation to each person. Enthronement is not a one-time act but a way of life. Its impact is a day-by-day, unfolding experience of Jesus's love.

Evangelization: Once we are touched and transformed by the love and mercy that flow from the Sacred Heart, we cannot keep it to ourselves. Our desire is to make his heart known and loved by as many people as possible. Thus, lay promoters of the enthronement play a vital role in spreading devotion to the Sacred Heart. Fr. Mateo could not have carried out his mission of the social reign of the Sacred Heart without the help of lay promoters. Enthronement is a ministry in itself. It is a call to live out the promises of the Sacred Heart and lead others to the remedy of love that this devotion provides.

The Role of Children in Enthronements and in Sacred Heart Devotion

Fr. Mateo, from the very beginning of his worldwide work to promote the social reign of the Sacred Heart, recognized the vital role that children play in the apostolate. With their hearts not yet scarred or jaded, children can easily relate to and conceive of Jesus as King of their homes. In fact, Fr. Mateo's first chosen "apostles of enthronement" were children just eight and ten years old.

For many of the people whose stories are contained here, devotion to the Sacred Heart began when they were children. The image hanging in their family homes invited conversation. And these conversations led them to know the King of their homes as the King of their hearts!

To nurture this devotion in children, Fr. Mateo formed, with ecclesiastical approval, the League of Tarcisius (also known as the League of Tarcisians). St. Tarcisius was a twelve-year-old boy who lived during the time of the Roman persecutions. He was a very devout young man with a particular love for Jesus in the Eucharist. One day, he was secretly taking the Eucharist to imprisoned Christians. Jesus was tucked safely in a bundle under his cloak, near his heart. When a group of Roman boys demanded this package, Tarcisius refused, and the boys beat him to death. This young martyr has been an inspiration to youth throughout the ages.

The League of Tarcisius was founded:

> [F]or the purpose of grouping boys and girls together into a zealous band of apostles of the Sacred Heart, especially to promote the Reign of the Sacred Heart in homes and in society, through the Enthronement of the Sacred Heart in the home.

Thus it is essentially, and in the first place, an apostolate, and auxiliary instrument to the Work of the Enthronement.[5]

The league encourages the offering of "three golden pennies" of prayer for souls: little sacrifices (especially obedience), attending weekly Mass, and receiving Communion worthily.

Establishing a chapter of the League of Tarcisius is a natural extension of the Catholic school or home school experience, but it can also be associated with parish life and faith formation. Father John A. Hardon, Servant of God and a spiritual leader of modern times, wrote extensively on devotion to the Sacred Heart. He noted:

> A number of sisters have found Fr. Mateo's League of Tarcisians highly practicable.... One teacher writes, "We began our League early in January, giving the aspirants a probation period of four months. About 65% of the children in grades 4 to 6 responded. At the end of the probation, about 40% had remained faithful. Solemn enrollment took place on the First Friday in May. Each Tarcisian received a special program with dates for group Mass attendance, directions for depositing their sacrifice records, and pertinent information. One index of success is the children's fidelity to Mass and Holy Communion during the summer months.[6]

The simple yet profound and foundational concepts of prayer, sacrifice, and love of the Eucharist are especially appealing to children and youth when they are presented in the right way and with the intention of love. Little ones love to please, and young adults embrace the truth and reality of the promises with their impressionable and idealistic hearts. As the stories below will demonstrate, even today children are often leaders in devotion to the Sacred Heart within the home.

Healing Stories

Many families, even very loving ones, experience periods of extreme stress due to illness or addictions or a clash of wills. We may want to wait until everything is picture-perfect before having an enthronement, but if we did, there wouldn't be many of them! When everything is falling apart, that is exactly when Jesus wants to be in the home. He dwells within our messy lives.

One family in the preparation phase was barely speaking. Even as they were praying together, the tension was thick enough to cut with a knife. It was clear that between the father and teenaged son, all was *not* well; in fact, they barely acknowledged one another. The mother tried to make up for the awkward silences, but she couldn't hide the fact that there was a very difficult relationship between the two.

The father had grown harsh and difficult under the burden of almost constant and excruciating back pain. He was in the habit of lashing out at the family, and his sixteen-year-old son bore the brunt of his ire. The father seemed to unduly pick on the boy, with a demanding and rigid attitude toward him. The son withdrew and sometimes rebelled.

It was Christmastime when the entire family—father, mother, son, and extended family members—gathered for the enthronement. During the ceremony, participants are asked to offer petitions similar to those we offer at Mass. This is when the son spoke up. With a trembling voice, he prayed, "Lord, if you are *really* here, please heal my father. He is in a lot of pain, and I know that he doesn't mean all of the things he says."

Through this simple, heartfelt prayer, the son took the lead in forgiving his father. After a long moment, the father walked over to the son, with tears welling up in his eyes. No words were spoken; only a long embrace melted away years of painful words and actions and softened both of their hearts. With one single prayer, the young man led his family to the promise of Jesus's healing grace.

* * *

At a Sacred Heart mission in Louisiana, parishioners were learning about Enthronement of the Sacred Heart in their homes. Immediately following a presentation, the leader felt an urgent tugging on her sleeve and heard a little voice crying, "My mommy is sick, my mommy is sick!" Looking down, the leader saw a little boy, about nine years of age, filled with deep love and concern. He explained that his mother had cancer. The boy brought the leader to his parents and asked for prayer and Jesus's help to cure his mom. His faith was pure and strong.

The leader told the boy, "Nobody loves your mother as you do, so I want you to lay your hands on your mom while I talk to Jesus."

The mission continued for several days. On the last day, the little boy returned. He explained that his mother had been to the doctor, and the doctor said she was no longer sick. Her cancer had gone into "rest" (remission)! Shining with joy, as if he had just come down from heaven, the little boy could not wait to tell everyone what Jesus had done.

This childlike trust is what Jesus desires of us: "Unless you turn and become like children, you will not enter the kingdom of heaven. Whoever humbles himself like this child is the greatest in the kingdom of heaven" (Matthew 18:3–4).

♥ *Heart Note* ♥

Jesus said, "Unless you turn and become like children." This indicates that we must put some effort into being changed. Some of the characteristics of a hard heart are bitterness, unforgiveness, jealousy, cynicism, pride, and vanity. The childlike heart conditions are joy, mercy, generosity of spirit, hope, desire for God, humility, and purity of intention.

Ask the Sacred Heart to guide you in making that "turn." Ask him to make your heart truly childlike and ready for the kingdom of God.

Sacred Heart of Jesus, Thy Kingdom come!

Chapter Eight

Mary, Mother of the Sacred Heart

The Immaculate Heart of Mary and the Sacred Heart of Jesus are eternally entwined. Some people combine the two devotions, but there is an important distinction between them.

The devotion to the Sacred Heart of Jesus is especially directed to the "Divine Heart," as overflowing with love for humanity. In the devotion to the Immaculate Heart of Mary, on the other hand, the attraction is the love of her Immaculate Heart for Jesus and for God.

> In devotion to the Immaculate Heart of Mary...love is more the result than the "object" of the devotion; the object being rather to love God and Jesus by uniting oneself to Mary for this purpose and by imitating her virtues to help one achieve this.[1]

As mentioned in chapter six, the Feast of the Immaculate Heart of Mary is celebrated the day after the Feast of the Sacred Heart. Devotion to Mary's Heart can be traced back to the early Church. In the seventeenth century, St. John Eudes helped fuel the devotion, observing February 8 as the Feast of the Immaculate Heart of Mary some twenty years before a Feast for the Sacred Heart was established. (Again, Mary prepares the way and leads us to her son.) Both Pope Leo XIII and Pope St. Pius X called St. John Eudes "the father, Doctor, and Apostle of the liturgical cult of the Sacred Hearts of Jesus and Mary."[2]

Devotion to the Immaculate Heart of Mary is closely associated with her appearances in Paris in 1830 to St. Catherine Labouré, then a young novice with the Daughters of Charity. Through those apparitions, the Blessed Mother instructed the faithful to wear a medal, known as the Miraculous Medal, to remind us of her constant love and protection. There are many powerful stories of conversion and heavenly help associated with this popular sacramental.[3]

The Immaculate Heart of Mary is most often shown encircled with flowers, representing her virtue and purity, and pierced with a sword, commemorating Simeon's words to her, "A sword will pierce your own soul too," at the presentation of Jesus (Luke 2:35). Mary's sorrow extends to compassion for humanity; she suffers with us as our Sorrowful Mother. She is also our Merciful Mother, loving all sinners. She is Our Lady of Perpetual Help, ever ready to shower us with her graces and intercede for us before the throne of her son.

The physical heart of Mary is not the sole object of the devotion. Her spiritual heart is also for our imitation. We are told more than once in Scripture that Mary kept and pondered things in her heart (see Luke 2:19, 51). The interior life of Mary was singularly focused on the love and will of God. She lived in submission and receptivity to all that God had for her. Her *fiat*, "Be it done unto me according to your word," lived out day by day, is our example of total trust in the Sacred Heart of Jesus.

THE FATIMA MESSAGE

A more recent outpouring of devotion to the Immaculate Heart of Mary flows from Our Lady's appearances in Fatima, Portugal, from May 13 to October 17, 1917. Our Lady appeared to three children, Jacinto and Francisco Marto and Lucia Dos Santos, and delivered a message: God wanted to save poor sinners through worldwide devotion to her Immaculate Heart. The Fatima message is similar to the mission of the reign of the Sacred Heart: to increase prayer and to offer sacrifices and reparation to God for the many offenses against him. Our Lady is urging us to love her son through her Immaculate Heart and to save souls through our prayer and devotion.

There are four parts to the devotion requested by the Blessed Mother in her appearances to the children of Fatima. All of them are to be carried out in a spirit of reparation and a desire for world peace.

1. Go to confession eight days before or after the First Saturday of the month.
2. Receive Holy Communion on five consecutive First Saturdays of the month.
3. Pray a daily rosary.
4. Meditate for at least fifteen minutes on the mysteries of the Holy rosary.

Our Lady told Lucia that she would assist at the hour of death anyone who followed through on her request. The five Saturdays represent particular outrages against her Immaculate Heart: offenses against her Immaculate Conception, against her virginity, against her divine maternity, by those who openly seek to inspire indifference or hatred for the Immaculate Heart, and by those who directly disparage her holy images.

These sacrileges seem to be alive and flourishing in our society today. Consider the culture of death in which we live, with its disregard for chaste living, coupled with the overt and outrageous depictions of Our Lady in modern so-called art. We would do well to make reparation for all of this and more.

Neither Mary nor Jesus has a drop of condemnation in their Hearts. They foresaw our current troubles and seek simple ways to aid us. The devotions to the Immaculate Heart of Mary and the Sacred Heart of Jesus are meant to fortify us and assist us on our way to heaven, to be with them for all eternity.

To Jesus through Mary

Total Consecration to Jesus through Mary is a very powerful and efficacious devotion that was put forth by St. Louis de Montfort (1673–1716) in a classic book entitled *True Devotion to the Blessed Virgin Mary*. The consecration has been revived and modernized recently by the Marian Fathers of the Immaculate Conception, also known as the Divine Mercy Fathers, through a book by Father Michael Gaitley, *33 Days to Morning Glory*. Both books offer a thirty-three–day period of spiritual preparation and exercises in anticipation of consecration, when a person fully offers himself or herself to Jesus through the merits of Mary's Immaculate Heart.

According to a publication of the Montfort Fathers,

> Saint Louis de Montfort promoted and spread devotion to the Sacred Heart of Jesus to a far greater extent than is generally realized. The silence of his biographers on this subject is surprising, not to say baffling. It is especially surprising when one considers the fact that his hymns on the Sacred Heart number no fewer than 905 lines; this is to say nothing of the mention he makes of the Heart of Christ in his other writings.[4]

Currently, the *33 Days to Morning Glory* retreats, offered through the Hearts Afire Parish programs, are having a profound effect on the hearts of many faithful. The Marian Fathers of the Immaculate Conception make it clear that they focus on consecration through the Immaculate Heart of Mary because it always leads us to the Sacred Heart of Jesus. Fr. Gaitley articulates this in his book and retreat program entitled *Consoling the Heart of Jesus*.

I can attest to this. I and a small group of friends completed our retreat and consecrated ourselves to Jesus through Mary on the Feast of our Lady of Guadalupe, December 12, 2014. I had no indication of what was to come, yet within seven months, I was working with the Sacred Heart Apostolate and was contracted to write this book!

Below is another story of how the two devotions work in concert, just as the two hearts beat together for us all.

A Consecration Story

Dominic and Ginger made a total consecration to Jesus through Mary while they were in college. They went on to fully embrace their Catholic faith. They have now been married for over twenty years and have eight children. Dominic explains that it was the consecration that led them to discover and embrace devotion to the Sacred Heart early in their marriage. "The Blessed Mother always leads us to the heart of her Son." He attributes his family's happiness and spiritual health to both these devotions.

Dominic does not sugarcoat the anxieties, especially financial ones, that creep in when raising a large family. There are also the pressures of trying to stay present and maintain open communication with Ginger, who home schools their children. Nevertheless, the Sacred Heart of Jesus has provided for them every step of the way. Following on their own home enthronement, they actively promote home enthronements in their parish. At the time of this writing, twenty families have signed up!

Dominic explains that the devotion helps the entire family, especially the children, to be faithful witnesses to the love of Christ and his centrality in their lives. Extended family members who are not religious have remarked on how helpful and well-behaved the children are (for the most part!), a fact that Dominic attributes to Ginger and the Sacred Heart:

> The one thing that I can point to is the overall harmony that exists in our home—especially with the kids. I see Jesus in these

kids, and so do others! The spiritual wealth we have is a witness of joy that wouldn't be there without the Sacred Heart.

Dominic's job takes him away from the family some evenings. He is grateful that in his absence, he has the assurance that the Lord is always present in his home. For every family member, but especially for Ginger, Jesus is a friend and a refuge. Being a homeschooling mom is not easy, and she entrusts her anxieties and concerns to the Sacred Heart on a regular basis, often with the words *I can't do this!*

Dominic stresses the fact that they are *not* a perfect family. The fruits of consecration to the Immaculate Heart of Mary and devotion to the Sacred Heart are an overwhelming sense of gratitude and an unwavering trust that God will always provide what he and his family need.

* * *

It is good to invite Mary to join us in our devotion to the heart of her son, for a mother always knows best the heart of her child. Through devotion to the Immaculate Heart, a path is cleared to the Sacred Heart of Jesus. The two hearts together are an unbeatable team!

♥ *Heart Note* ♥

How might you invite Mary to be a part of your devotion to the Sacred Heart? What way are you being called to honor Mary's Immaculate Heart?

Sacred Hearts of Jesus and Mary, be forever praised!

Chapter Nine

Divine Mercy and the Sacred Heart

One of the most popular and growing devotions in the Church today is the devotion to the Divine Mercy. It is based on the private revelations and apparitions of Our Lord to a Polish Sister of Our Lady of Mercy, St. Faustina Kowalska. She became the first saint of the third millennium, and Pope John Paul II declared her the great Apostle of Divine Mercy for our times.

The two devotions—Divine Mercy and Sacred Heart—can be said to be two facets of a brilliant diamond that is the heart of Jesus. Each incorporates a divinely inspired image with an urgent message for the world. There are distinctions between them as well.

Between 1931 and 1938, the Lord appeared to Sr. Faustina Kowalska and delivered his message of mercy for our times. He asked her to record in a diary all that he told her, and that work is entitled *Diary: Divine Mercy in My Soul.* Even though St. Faustina had only three years of formal education, she produced this volume of over seven hundred pages of deep mystical writings of theological precision.

The message is a continuation of the dialogue of Jesus's heart:

> My Heart overflows with great mercy for souls, and especially for poor sinners.... It is for them that the Blood and Water flowed from My Heart as from a fount overflowing with mercy. For them I dwell in the tabernacle as King of Mercy.[1]

As with the devotion to the Sacred Heart, Jesus requested specific practices, prayers, and feasts to be instituted, to draw souls to his merciful heart. The well-known image shows Jesus touching his glowing chest, from which two rays emanate, one red and the other white. Jesus told Sr. Faustina that he wanted the painting inscribed with a signature: "Jesus, I Trust in You."

Jesus asked that the image be blessed on the first Sunday after Easter, which he instituted as the Feast of Divine Mercy. (This is similar to his calling centuries before for the Feast of the Sacred Heart.) The Lord said, "By means of this image I shall be granting many graces to souls; so let every soul have access to it." [2]

There are other aspects of the Divine Mercy devotion that parallel the Sacred Heart devotion. For example, Jesus requested a special time of prayer: He asked St. Margaret Mary to accompany him on Thursday nights between the hours of 11 PM and midnight as a consolation for his suffering in Gethsemane; the Divine Mercy devotion includes accompanying the Savior every day between 3 PM and 4 PM, the hour of his passion, when he poured out his mercy and his life to save us all.

The Lord also indicated that certain prayers and practices should accompany each devotion. First Friday observances are part of the Sacred Heart devotion; the Divine Mercy devotion includes the recitation of the Chaplet of Divine Mercy. Both devotions also make promises to those who practice them and call for lives of holiness centered on Eucharistic charity and trust in Jesus.

What is the relationship between the two devotions? Dr. Robert Stackpole, director of the John Paul II Institute of Divine Mercy, explains:

> Devotion to the Sacred Heart may be defined as the worship and service of the Second Person incarnate of the Holy Trinity, Jesus Christ, because of His love for us, symbolized by His pierced and wounded Heart of flesh. Devotion to The Divine

Mercy, on the other hand, may be defined as the worship and service of the Triune God, because of His merciful love for us, poured out through the Merciful Heart of Jesus, and symbolized by the rays that stream from His breast in the Mercy Image. The centrality of the Heart of Jesus in both devotions is clearly evident.[3]

It is wholly appropriate and even desirable to practice both devotions. Consider that in devotion to the Sacred Heart, we focus on what we give to Jesus: love, consolation, and reparation expressed through sincere and contrite hearts, sorrowful for the sins that we have committed. With the Divine Mercy devotion, the focus is on what we get from Jesus: his unfailing mercy. It is obvious why the devotion to the Sacred Heart came first. We can only ask for and receive his mercy to the extent that we are aware of how much we need it. As in any good and solid relationship, there must be a give and take. The two devotions are balanced on the fulcrum of his Heart!

One priest commented, "Your heart, Lord, is the only hospital door we need knock on. You are the only physician the Father endorses and certifies as capable of healing us."[4] In fact, Jesus seemed to make the relationship of the two devotions clear when he spoke to St. Faustina, who also had a devotion to the Sacred Heart:

My mercy is greater than your sins and those of the entire world.... I let My Sacred Heart be pierced with a lance, thus opening wide the source of mercy for you. Come then, with trust to draw graces from this fountain. [5]

And:

Gaze on my Heart filled with goodness and imbued with My sentiments. Strive for meekness and humility; be merciful to others, as I am to you; and when you feel your strength failing, if you come to the fountain of mercy to fortify your soul, you will not grow weary on your journey.[6]

A Healing Story

Laura's story reflects how the two devotions in tandem can bring forth great healing. Laura is a brilliant and devout woman who struggles with mental illness. Now in her sixties, she has endured rejection and broken relationships because of that diagnosis. She has experienced countless hospitalizations and disastrous repercussions from drugs that were supposed to help her.

One of the most difficult challenges Laura faces with her condition is a tendency toward scrupulosity. She often feels that her illness is a moral weakness that God finds offensive and unforgiveable. As a result, she battles mental torment and depression, fearing that she is outside of God's mercy and loving embrace.

Laura has always been deeply devoted to the Sacred Heart. She is quick to make reparation for her sins and relates very personally to the thorns that encircle the heart of Jesus. She understands the pain, insult, and mockery they represent.

One day, Laura called me on the phone with jubilance evident in her voice. A priest from whom she received spiritual direction had broken through the scrupulosity with an image and exercise that reflect the gift of Divine Mercy and the promise of the Sacred Heart. The priest instructed her to take every fault and failing (perceived or actual) that was troubling her and to mentally place it into the wound in Christ's side, the one that appears on his heart and that he invited Thomas to probe. The priest then invited Laura to imagine herself as the penitent woman, soaking the feet of Jesus with her tears, or as Mary Magdalene at the foot of the cross. The priest guided Laura to imagine the rays of Divine Mercy flowing directly from Jesus and completely showering her.

As the rays covered her, Laura offered all of her weaknesses, imperfections, inabilities, and sins to Jesus—just as she might *bring a gift to a friend.* Each pain, each sorrow, each repeated weakness, and each interior struggle became a precious offering to Jesus, to use for his good purposes. And the next part was the key: *to trust him to do it.* JESUS, I TRUST IN YOU!

Laura learned, by God's grace, that we don't have to be great saints to receive his mercy, only trusting little souls. He does not seek perfect souls but loving ones. And for him, our every act of trust is like a butterfly kiss upon his Most Sacred Heart!

When we trust in God's mercy, we take our meager offerings, even our sufferings and weaknesses, and give them to the Lord. We leave them with him, so that he can make something beautiful and good from them, as only he can. This is the work of his heart and the purpose of his passion. Our trust in his ability to take our misery and bring about a greater good inspires the endless flow of mercy from his sacred side.

♥ *Heart Note* ♥

How is Jesus inviting you to receive the gift of his mercy into your life and heart? Who might you share this mercy with?

Sweet Merciful Heart of Jesus, save us..

Chapter Ten

A Devotion for All Times

The Sacred Heart devotion has waxed and waned in popularity over the years, but it will never die. It expresses the deepest desire of God for each one of us: to know his heart. Recent popes and spiritual leaders have spoken and written at length of the benefits of the devotion. They share a sense of urgency to provide solid teachings and encourage spiritual practices that are rooted in truth and love.

In 1956, Pope Pius XII delivered his Encyclical on Devotion to the Sacred Heart (*Haurietis Aquas*) to defend and promote the worldwide devotion to the Sacred Heart. He encouraged the faithful:

> We…urge all children in Christ, both those who are already accustomed to drink the saving waters flowing from the Heart of the Redeemer and, more especially, those who look on from a distance like hesitant spectators, to eagerly embrace this devotion. Let them carefully consider…that it is a…devotion which has long been powerful in the Church and is solidly founded on the Gospel narrative….
>
> Moreover, there are…the abundant and joyous fruits which have flowed…to the Church: countless souls returned to the Christian religion, the faith of many roused to greater activity, a closer tie between the faithful and our most loving Redeemer. All these benefits, particularly in the most recent decades, have passed before our eyes in greater numbers and more dazzling significance.[1]

Pope St. John Paul II, known as "the Mercy Pope," championed devotion to the Sacred Heart throughout his pontificate. His love for the devotion was nurtured from his boyhood in Poland. From 1985 to 1989, the pope devoted his Sunday Angelus messages to the Litany of the Sacred Heart, delivering thirty-three reflections based on the thirty-three lines of the litany. Jesus lived thirty-three years, and each invocation contemplates a characteristic of his heart.

In a letter to Bishop Raymond Séguy on the three-hundredth anniversary of the death of St. Margaret Mary, in 1990, Pope John Paul II indicated that he prayed for a restoration of the veneration of the Sacred Heart by the faithful. "For it is in the Heart of Christ that the human heart learns to know the true and unique meaning of its life and destiny; it is in the Heart of Christ that the human heart receives its capacity to love."[2]

In 2001, Cardinal Raymond Leo Burke, then bishop of the diocese of La Crosse, Wisconsin, arranged for Enthronement of the Sacred Heart in every parish in his diocese. Bishop Burke stated that he was inspired by his own experience with devotion to the Sacred Heart from his childhood and motivated "by a great need among people for a devotion which would bring the Eucharist to the home—to enable the family to continue to live consciously in the presence of Christ at all times. In this way, Christ is recognized as the king of the heart, of the home, and as a constant member of the family."[3]

In 2011, at World Youth Day, Pope Benedict XVI consecrated the world's youth to the Sacred Heart of Jesus. Official teaching prior to the consecration pointed out that contemplation of the Sacred Heart of Jesus opens up new paths to holiness. This was the pope's prayer, a prayer that we can continue to pray today for our youth, who need much help in combating the temptations of the world:

> Lord Jesus Christ, Brother, Friend, and Redeemer of Mankind,
> look with love upon the youth gathered here,
> and open for them the eternal fountain of your mercy,

which flows from your open heart on the cross.
They have come to be with you and adore you.
With ardent prayer, I consecrate them to your Heart,
so that, rooted and built up in you,
they will always be yours, in life and in death.
May they never turn away from you!
Give them hearts like yours, meek and humble,
so that they may always listen to your voice and your commands,
do your will, and be praise to you throughout the world,
so that mankind, contemplating their works,
may give glory to the Father, with whom you live in everlasting
happiness,
in the unity of the Holy Spirit, forever and ever. Amen.[4]

Pope Francis, in an Angelus message, said: "The Heart of Jesus is the ultimate symbol of God's mercy. But it is not an imaginary symbol; it is a real symbol which represents the centre, the source from which salvation flowed for all of humanity."[5] Clearly, one cannot experience mercy without encountering the Sacred Heart from which it flows.

The Sacred Heart devotion weds the rich tradition of a foundational devotion with a remedy for our hurting world today. It holds forth the promises of Jesus, which can convert hearts and transform lives by moving us from distraction to devotion, from superficiality and sentimentality to authenticity, from materialism to sacrifice, from lukewarmness to a sincere desire to repair the damage done by our sins, from self-centeredness to interior freedom and the triumph of Love.

♥ Heart Note ♥

Contemplate how you might share the message of the Sacred Heart devotion with others who are hurting.

Most Sacred Heart of Jesus, be our light!

Part Three

A Heart
Full of
Promises

Chapter Eleven

The Promises

He promised me that all those who are devoted and consecrated to Him will never be lost. [1]
—St. Margaret Mary Alacoque

In many of Jesus's apparitions to St. Margaret Mary, he explained the
great rewards and promises that he so generously desired to extend
to those devoted to his Sacred Heart. One time he asked, "Do you
believe I can do this? If you believe, you will see the power of my
heart in the magnificence of my love." [2]

Today, it seems as though Jesus's promises are like unopened
gifts. Many have never heard of them; others have forgotten them
or stopped looking for their treasure in their lives. Jesus invites us
to grab hold of these promises and break them open with our faith.
He desires that our hearts expand, our faith increase, and our trust
in him and his loving and merciful heart grow beyond our imagin-
ings. As Fr. Larkin wrote in his seminal book *Enthronement of the
Sacred Heart*, "You have to have a lot of trust in the merciful love of
the Sacred Heart. *Confidence is the key to his heart.*" [3]

These promises, drawn from the writings of St. Margaret Mary,
do not represent the totality of what Jesus told her. They have been
listed in different ways throughout the ages with varying emphases.
The publication of the promises as we know them today "dates back
to 1882, when an American businessman from Dayton, Ohio, Philip
Kemper, distributed the list throughout the world." [4] It's worthy to note
that one of the hallmarks of those who are attracted to and spread the

devotion to the Sacred Heart is their littleness and their sanctification through ordinary occupations. The lay faithful have always been integral to the witness and promotion of devotion to the Sacred Heart.

As we come to know more and more about Jesus's heart, we realize the rich abundance of his promises to us, which seem to multiply like the loaves and the fishes (see Matthew 14:13–21). We honor Jesus when we humbly, gratefully, and eagerly accept all that he wants to give us, with faith and purity of heart. Let us ache for the heavenly support of his promises and delight in taking Jesus at his word.

St. Margaret Mary's words about the promises of this devotion speak to our longing hearts today:

> As to persons living in the world, they shall find in this devotion all the aids necessary in their state of life: peace in their homes, consolation in their work, the blessing of heaven upon all of their enterprises, comfort in their sorrows, a secure refuge during life and especially at the hours of death…. It is plainly evident that there is no one in the world who will not receive all kinds of heavenly blessings if they have a true love of Jesus Christ manifested by a devotion to the Sacred heart of Jesus.[5]

Here are the twelve promises to those who practice this devotion:

1. I will give them all the graces necessary in their state in life.
2. I will establish peace in their homes.
3. I will comfort them in all of their afflictions.
4. I will be their refuge in life and especially in death.
5. I will abundantly bless their undertakings.
6. Sinners will find in my heart the source and infinite ocean of mercy.
7. Lukewarm souls will become fervent.
8. Fervent souls shall quickly mount to high perfection.
9. I will bless those places wherein the image of my Sacred Heart

shall be exposed and honored.

10. I will give to priests the power to touch the most hardened hearts.

11. Those who shall promote this devotion shall have their names written in my heart.

12. I promise you in the excessive mercy of my Heart that my all-powerful love will grant to all those who receive Holy Communion on the First Fridays in nine consecutive months the grace of final perseverance; they shall not die in my disgrace, nor without receiving their sacraments. My divine Heart shall be their safe refuge in this last moment.

Can we believe these promises? Fr. Larkin would reply wholeheartedly:

> YES, for these reasons: 1) they have been approved and cited by the Church; 2) they have been fulfilled many times in the lives of all kinds of people; and 3) they are nothing else but an elaboration of the promises of Christ found in the Gospel.[6]

Fr. Larkin called the promises of the Sacred Heart "a hidden treasure" because so few know of their extent and variety. He points out that "the twelve promises do not begin to enumerate the promises made by our divine Lord…. They are not even a summary of them but rather a selection, chosen to inspire love for the Sacred Heart."[7] They are just the beginning of the never-ending pledges of love and faithfulness that flow from the Sacred Heart of Jesus.

St. Margaret Mary shares the deep desire of Jesus's heart with regard to his promises:

> One Friday, after I received our Lord in Holy Communion,… He clearly stated His wishes in this manner: "I *thirst*…. I have a burning thirst to be honored by men…. I find hardly anyone who endeavors, according to my desires, to quench that thirst by making some return to me."[8]

Dr. Thomas D. Williams explains, "This thirst of Jesus isn't some narcissistic need to be loved; Jesus craves our love because he wants to fill us with himself. He wants to give us a joy that we can know only by loving him. Jesus' thirst for love is a thirst *to give love*."[9]

Ultimately, the way that we quench the thirst of Jesus for love is to claim and believe his promises, take them into our hearts, and live them out in our day-to-day lives. When we do this, we bear witness to the great fire of his unending love for all. Many long for this love but don't know where or how to find it. Others struggle to believe. Jesus's heart is our refuge and remedy.

Jesus's twelve promises are real and everlasting. Each of the remaining chapters in this book is devoted to one of them. Each chapter contains personal stories of how Jesus has fulfilled these promises in the lives of people from various walks of life. At the end of each chapter are Bible verses in which the promise for that chapter can be found, for further contemplation.

What I found striking in the stories is that Jesus met people "right where they were." They did not have to exhibit extraordinary holiness or be particularly devout in order to interest him in sharing his heart with them. In fact, the tone of Jesus's message to St. Margaret Mary and to the whole world is one of deep longing for us to return to his love. Far from being judgmental, he wants us to trust in him and be genuinely grateful for all the ways in which he loves us.

♥ *Heart Note* ♥

Today, Jesus asks us the same question that he asked St. Margaret Mary: "Do you believe I can do this?" As you look at each of the twelve promises, consider what your answer will be to this question.

O Sacred Heart, we thank you, we adore you, and we claim your promises with an unshakeable confidence. Amen.

A Promise of Grace

I will give them all the graces necessary in their state of life.

A grace is a supernatural help from God. We can't earn graces; they are freely and generously given from his loving heart. However, we can work to make sure that we are disposed to receive them. This "work" that we do is to seek God with our whole mind, heart, soul, and strength; confess our sins regularly, so as not to be drawn down by them; make reparation for those sins, so that Jesus can bring good out of them; and *listen* to him through Scripture, in prayer, and at Mass.

Graces help us to lead lives of holiness and virtue, which not only is pleasing to God but is the only way that we can truly experience fulfillment and joy in our lives. In fact, at every stage of life, the Lord gives us the opportunity to claim his graces for the good of others and ourselves. St. Margaret Mary shows us how to claim them:

> Our Lord will grant you many graces if you have the courage to follow Him by entire self-forgetfulness, abandonment to His providence [holy will] and great purity of intention, always uniting yourself to the intentions of His Sacred Heart.[1]

One woman described it like this: "The devotion to the Sacred Heart of Jesus moves Jesus from our heads to our hearts."

We all have head knowledge of who Jesus is; the devotion helps us to know Jesus *with our hearts*. We are given the graces that we need to love him more and more. And when we encounter his love and remain open to receiving it, our hearts expand, and we are able to love others more as well.

♥ *Heart Note* ♥

What graces have you received lately? What graces do you still need? We need humility to ask for God's grace. Are there areas of your life where you try to "go it alone"? Here is a short prayer to ask for God's grace:

> Merciful Lord, you are never weary of speaking to my poor heart. Grant me grace that, if today I hear your voice, my heart may not be hardened. Amen.[2]

HEALING STORIES

A young mother with several small children struggled with anxiety. Most of her unsettledness stemmed from her perfectionist nature, which didn't blend well with the delightful messiness and chaotic nature of a household that includes little ones. She struggled to remain patient and kind in the presence of her children. The only relief came when they were at school, when she could gain comfort in getting everything "under control "and in perfect order.

Of course, everything would be undone when the children came home. This began to weigh on the mother's heart. Instead of welcoming her children with open arms, she dreaded their return each day and was filled with guilt because of it. She began taking a tranquilizer each afternoon as her children arrived home from school. She was only vaguely aware that she was getting dependent on the drug when she had an enthronement of the Sacred Heart in her home.

One day, shortly after the ceremony, the woman's nine-year-old daughter came bounding into the home. She was full of excitement as she called out to her mother, "Come on, Mommy. Don't you remember we are supposed to talk to Jesus and tell him everything?"

The little girl took her mother by the hand and led her to the image. She started telling Jesus all about her day at school, her friends, and what she had learned, chattering freely and sharing every detail. When the little girl indicated that it was now her mother's turn to speak, the woman couldn't. She was not accustomed to praying like that. So she shared a Hail Mary.

Day after day, the little girl brought her mother in front of the picture of Jesus on her arrival from school. Slowly the woman began to open up. At first the conversations were short and tentative, but over time the words began to flow. And eventually her dread was replaced with a sense of peace, her anxiety with a sense of joyful anticipation for her children to come home from school. She couldn't wait for her little girl to join her in their visit with Jesus!

"Not only did I find myself getting to know Jesus as he drew me closer to him; I was also becoming closer and deepening my relationship with my daughter." It was a complete turnaround, fueled by grace. The mother was able to give up the tranquilizers; she no longer needed or wanted pills to cope with life. Pursuit of perfection gave way to living in the present moment. Now she could be the mother she wanted to be. Through the Sacred Heart of Jesus, she grew to delight in her children and her Lord

* * *

A woman of advanced age, a widow, attended a Sacred Heart Mission at her church. The mission lasted several days, and many "seasoned citizens" and a few young families were there to learn about the Sacred Heart devotion and enthroning their homes (and their parish) to the Sacred Heart. This woman, who was a nurse, was struggling with health issues and feelings of uselessness. Her whole life had been devoted to helping others, and now she seemed all alone at a time when she needed help herself.

She questioned whether as a single person she should even enthrone her home. The encouragement to have other family members be present troubled her, because she could think of no one who would be available to attend. When she approached the mission director on this, the heaviness of her heart came out in her voice. The admission that she was all alone was painful.

The mission director said, "I hope you sign up for an enthronement, because you won't be alone anymore!" She instructed her to hang the portrait of the Sacred Heart of Jesus in her home and to just sit still, looking at Jesus looking back at her. "It could take days, weeks, months, or years, but the more time you spend with Jesus and his Sacred Heart, and the more you practice with prayers the spirit of the enthronement, the less alone you will be."

The woman responded with some measure of hope but also with a sense that there was a deeper hurt that needed to be healed. "Maybe then he will take away my lonesomeness." What the mission director knew, because she had witnessed it countless times before, was that the deep wound of loneliness was soon to be healed by the presence of Jesus. She knew that Jesus *always meets us at the broken places.*

We all have wounds that need healing. And like Jesus, we carry them with us. It's Jesus who can stop the bleeding, but we have to invite him in. May we all be like this widow, who eventually had an enthronement in her home. Let us *sit still* and see what happens when Jesus shows up. (An enthronement ceremony for singles is available.)

* * *

The first encounter that Linda can remember with the Sacred Heart of Jesus was when she made her First Communion at the age of eight. She had always been drawn to a magnificent statue of Jesus pointing to his heart, which stood near a side altar in her church. She often prayed before that statue, especially moved by the lifelike blue eyes that gazed back at her. On that special day when she first received Jesus in the Eucharist, Linda made a point of stopping to pray with "her Jesus."

Throughout her childhood and into adulthood, Linda prayed many prayers to the Sacred Heart and spent many hours before the statue. When her wedding day came, Linda stood in the back of the church of her youth and fixed her eyes on the eyes of the statue. She made a silent vow to Jesus that she would be the best wife she could. She begged for the grace to be true to the vow she was about to make.

Linda would need that grace. The marriage was a difficult one, even after the birth of two lovely daughters and with the comfortable living that her husband provided. The two strong personalities often clashed, and alcohol sometimes fueled the strife. On one particular evening, the fighting was such that Linda decided she had had enough.

Linda's plan was to go to Mass the next morning and then proceed to the lawyer's office. She prayed in anguish during that Mass, wrestling with anger, pain, and fear. As she left the church of her youth, she noticed in the vestibule the Sacred Heart statue staring back at her. It had been moved to the entrance of the church, to the exact spot where Linda had stood before walking down the aisle to marry Dan.

Overwhelmed by the gaze of Jesus and the realization of where she was, Linda sat down on a step at the foot of the statue and sobbed. It was a long time before she could admit to Jesus, "I'm finished; this marriage is over." Amid her protestations, she heard a small voice in her heart say, "Do it for my sake. Do it for me."

A flood of memories came back to Linda, of the vow she made on her wedding day and of the many prayers she had prayed throughout her life for help from the Sacred Heart of Jesus. She realized there was only one course of action to take, and she took it—for him.

Linda and Dan have been married for forty-one years now and are enjoying retirement and their growing family. Life is still not without its problems, but Linda is quick to say, "The Sacred Heart saved my marriage."

* * *

Preservation of the sanctity of marriage and strength to live out the vows of holy matrimony; protection and assistance in upholding the sacredness of the family; keeping the family together and holy under the watchful eyes of our loving Lord and friend; knowing our true purpose and the love of God for us at every stage of life—all these come under this first promise.

We all need grace to fulfill our obligations in life. The heart of Jesus is the sure place from which this grace flows.

Promise One in Scripture

> With joy you will draw water from the wells of salvation. (Isaiah 12:3)

> From his fullness we have all received, grace upon grace. (John 1:16)

> But each of us was given grace according to the measure of Christ's gift. (Ephesians 4:7)

O Heart of Love, we place all our trust in you, for we fear all things from our own weakness but hope for all things from your goodness. Amen.

Chapter Thirteen

A Promise of Peace

I will establish peace in their homes.

St. Paul describes "the peace of God" as one that "surpasses all understanding" and that "will guard [our] hearts and minds in Christ Jesus" (Philippians 4:7). How many of us are longing for this kind of peace in our homes?

Vatican II spoke of the family as the "domestic church."[1] It is within the family that we are to nurture the presence of Christ. It is there that each member can encounter him. "The family has the mission to guard, reveal and communicate love," Pope John Paul II wrote in *Familiaris Consortio.*[2]

While Jesus intends our homes to be sanctuaries of his love, some are battlegrounds of strife and pain or of silence, of distance and disappointment. Let's allow this second promise to grip our hearts as we struggle against the forces that seek to break our families apart. The Sacred Heart of Jesus can inspire us and give us the strength to carry out the vital mission of the domestic church.

St. Margaret Mary gives us hope and inspiration for our families and our lives.

> What joy to belong entirely to God, to make one's dwelling in Him, and to lay in Him the basis of one's perfection. In Him the soul enjoys a reign of imperturbable peace, where it beholds the vicissitudes and events of life without being perturbed or disturbed by them....[3]

When we make Jesus King of our hearts and our homes, he doesn't take away all of our problems, but he does give us grace and peace of mind and soul beyond what the world can give.

HEALING STORIES

Sandra, who grew up in a traditionally Catholic home, married Tim, who was not Catholic. In fact, Tim's upbringing and the church that formed him held some strong biases against the teachings of the Catholic Church, based on historical misunderstandings and inaccuracies. Not wanting to "stir the pot," Sandra attended services of both faith traditions, even as they were raising their two sons. She prayed fervently but privately for a conversion of heart for her husband.

One Sunday morning, Tim noticed smoke coming from a wall in the dining room. He acted quickly, and the fire department was soon on the scene. Once the fire was out, a tapestry remained intact on the damaged wall. It had been a gift from Tim's pastor, who didn't know what to do with it because it was a large picture of the Sacred Heart of Jesus! Before leaving that day, the fireman pointed to the picture and said, "Someone was watching over you!"

Many years later, Sandra attended a Sacred Heart Congress in a nearby town. Something that was said that weekend struck a chord deep inside her: "*Everybody needs something, and the Sacred Heart wants to provide for you. The promises are for you and your family.*"

For Sandra and her family, there were two pressing needs: The first was the conversion of Tim and spiritual unity in the family; the second was release from an ongoing financial cross, brought on by a medical condition that limited Tim's ability to work.

Sandra left the conference with a burning desire in her heart to bring Jesus into her home. After praying to the Blessed Mother, she asked Tim if he would be open to a home enthronement of the

Sacred Heart. To her surprise, he agreed, "as long as I don't have to do anything!"

During the preparation time, promoters brought to the home a large traveling statue of Our Lady of Fatima. Sandra was convinced that Tim would surely shut the door on that, but he didn't. The Blessed Mother was welcomed into the kitchen, where she remained until the day of the enthronement.

The final hurdle for Sandra was finding the right image of the Sacred Heart to enthrone. She wanted something appropriately sensitive to Tim. The evening before the scheduled enthronement, no suitable image had been found. Sandra was trusting Jesus and the Blessed Mother completely, because they had worked so many minor miracles already.

When Sandra tucked her sons into bed that night, there was the image, staring her in the face! The tapestry from the dining room, saved from the fire years earlier, had been moved to the boys' room, where it hung unnoticed and forgotten. When Sandra presented it to Tim, he had no objections. After all, it had been a gift from his pastor. It was no doubt a divinely arranged image to unite this family!

The miracles did not stop. A "holy fire" was ignited within the family. Immediately after the enthronement, the boys insisted on having their bedroom enthroned, and a short ceremony was conducted. One of those little boys is a priest today.

One year after the enthronements, the family was blessed with a baby girl. She now works in the Youth and Young Adult Ministry Office of her diocese. As for Tim, he is a daily communicant and a Knight of Columbus, and he loves his Catholic faith.

Sandra says that one of the greatest blessings of their devotion to the Sacred Heart is the promise of peace in her family in the face of trials. The financial cross remains, but by God's grace, all three children went to college, and the family has traveled around the world with various apostolates and a music ministry with which they are involved.

"We have a deep understanding of the grace that comes with his promise of peace," Sandra says. "It is hard to describe the level of peace that I experience when I trust in the Sacred Heart...with all the decisions we make. With the image, I remember that *he is here*. When people come into our home, they know that we follow and love Christ."

Jesus is true to his word. He will never stop watching over Sandra and her family.

* * *

Steve and Claudia had been extremely excited in preparing for their baby daughter after several years of infertility. She was their "little miracle," and they had her name picked out: Mikayla, which means "gift from God." But complications arose during the birth, and a tragic mistake at the hospital left them childless once again. Both Claudia and Steve were inconsolable, understandably overwhelmed with grief.

Over time, Claudia found great comfort in her faith, while Steve pulled away. He grew angry and distant. Even the birth of a second daughter did not heal the deep emotional and spiritual wounds in his heart. While it may have looked on the outside as if all was well with the family, Claudia carried a heavy burden of sorrow over the explosive rage that had become a hallmark of Steve's interactions with others, including his daughter.

Claudia never lost her faith. She poured love into the wound that seemed to overwhelm Steve and infect the family. She was determined to keep her family together, even as she struggled with feelings of bitterness and rejection. She leaned on her relationship with the Lord to get her through. Still, the distance between her husband and their daughter broke her heart.

When Claudia heard about enthronement to the Sacred Heart, she knew that her family needed it desperately but that her husband would never consent. Most enthronement ceremonies encourage the husband, as head of the household, to take a lead role, be present, or at least consent to the enthronement. Each time Claudia approached Steve about it, he angrily refused. Claudia remained patient.

As their daughter grew, Claudia was busy with life. The family experienced the regular ups and downs brought on by the teenage years. Yet every now and again, Claudia would approach the topic of enthronement, until one time Steve said, "Go ahead and do it, but not when I'm around."

Claudia claimed this as a minor miracle! Nevertheless, she still did not want to go ahead with the enthronement without the participation of her husband. She placed an image of the Sacred Heart in a prominent place in their home, prayed, and said no more about the enthronement.

Once the image was up, Claudia noticed a definite shift in the climate of their home. There was a decrease in Steve's angry outbursts and even a sprinkling of laughter. Their daughter, who had been spending a lot of time outside of the home, was now very present. The family started eating meals together for the first time in years!

Now Claudia experiences a different kind of ache in her heart. It is an ache of gratitude and love for all the Sacred Heart is doing in her family, as she carries with her a quiet and joyful anticipation of what is to come.

* * *

♥ *Heart Note* ♥

How can you turn your home into a domestic church? Even if you live alone, Jesus can create an atmosphere of love and inclusion of his presence. Just ask him to show you the way.

Promise Two in Scripture

Those of steadfast mind you keep in peace—
   in peace because they trust in you. (Isaiah 26:3)

Glory to God in the highest heaven,
   and on earth peace among those whom he favors!
(Luke 2:14)

Do not worry about anything, but in everything by prayer and supplication with thanksgiving let your requests be made known to God. And the peace of God, which surpasses all understanding, will guard your hearts and your minds in Christ Jesus. (Philippians 4:6–7)

O Sacred Heart of Jesus, let your peace reign in my heart and in my home.

Chapter Fourteen

A Promise of Comfort

I will comfort them in all their afflictions.

How many of us feel that our lives are devoid of hope? Perhaps a marriage is on life support, or a relationship with a child seems hopelessly severed. Loneliness is a burden for many. Some people suffer silently; even those closest to them do not know that their hearts are aching. But Jesus knows.

What if we invite Jesus to come into our home? What happens when we open the door to find hope standing before us? St. Margaret Mary, with her intimate knowledge of Jesus and his Heart, shares these words that encourage us still today:

> Should you find yourself overwhelmed by fear, cast yourself into the abyss of the unshaken confidence of the Sacred Heart, and there your fear will give place to love. If you find yourself frail and weak, lapsing into faults at every moment, go to the Sacred Heart and draw from It the strength which will invigorate and revive you....
>
> If you are overwhelmed by sadness, go and plunge your soul into the ocean of the divine joy of the Sacred Heart.... One of the ways most pleasing to God...is to enter into the Sacred Heart of Jesus and to commit to Him all the cares of ourselves.[1]

HEALING STORIES

Here is a story of a family that was faltering in hope.

The husband had left his family for greener pastures. His wife was devastated. In the midst of her own hurt and grief, she tried to cope with her two college-age sons' reactions. They were deeply angered and disgusted by the actions of their father.

The mother had been to a home enthronement of the Sacred Heart at one of her neighbors', and she was convinced that her family needed the Sacred Heart. When she approached her sons about it, they laughed at her. "Do you really think that a ceremony of hanging a picture of the Sacred Heart will make things all right?" they asked. Neither one of the boys was aware of Jesus's promise to bring comfort to them in times of trial and affliction.

But the mother's faith was strong. She had seen proof already in the way that Jesus had helped her neighbor. She knew in her heart that there was reason to hope in the Heart of Jesus. She began to prepare for an enthronement.

The boys continued with their excuses why they would not join her: After all, it was summer time, and they had their own things planned. Nevertheless, they watched their mom get ready. They could tell that she was serious about this invitation to bring Jesus into their home. Seeing her taking this on by herself, they decided to help get the house ready for the guests who would be attending the enthronement. Families from the neighborhood attended each other's enthronements, so they anticipated a crowd.

The boys cleaned windows, did some small outside painting, and mowed the lawn. They invited a few friends to give them a hand. As they worked, the boys shared why they were doing all of this. Of course, they thought they were doing this for their mom, and indeed they were. Did they realize it was also for them?

The time of preparation for the enthronement brought both comfort and healing to the boys, and when the night came for the enthronement, they stepped up to the plate! They informed their mom that they would be there and that they had even asked a few of their friends. Of course, Mom was delighted.

People from throughout the neighborhood came. The mom had set up a beautiful sacred space for Jesus. Tears were flowing as one of the sons carried several pictures to place next to the image. They were pictures of their dad—one showed the boys with their father on a fishing trip, and another showed the mother with her husband in happier times. It was evident that the Sacred Heart had already begun to do something very special in their home and hearts.

At the very end of the evening, the doorbell rang. The enthronement facilitator was on her way out, so she went with the mom to answer the door. The mom was jubilantly expressing her gratitude for the role her sons had played in the event.

Still chatting, the women opened the door. They were stunned to see the mother's husband standing there. "Hello," he said. "Is everything all right? I have driven around the house several times, trying to get enough courage to face you. And every time I would go by, there seemed to be more cars...." Before his wife could answer, the man asked for forgiveness.

The facilitator quickly slipped through the door. She turned to see through the large picture window an incredible scene. The boys were leaping up and running to their dad, dragging him and his suitcase into the house. The wife linked arms with her husband as they all gathered around the picture of the Sacred Heart of Jesus. Together the mother and the young men were introducing the father to their special Visitor, explaining what had just happened in their home.

Several days later, the facilitator received a call from the woman, who wanted to know how she could proclaim this good news. Her family was back together! The mother belonged to a group called Theresians International, a women's ministry that follows the little way of St. Thérèse. Eventually she was able to share her family's story in the organization's newsletter. She shared how Jesus comforted her family in the midst of their deepest turmoil and how the Heart of Jesus reached in to heal the broken hearts of her sons. She explained that, when invited, Jesus comes and breathes new life and love into our families.

* * *

Evie has loved the Sacred Heart of Jesus for as long as she can remember. Now in her sixties, she endured a difficult and lonely childhood due to an obvious facial deformity. Many of her classmates shunned her, and her brothers and sisters were embarrassed by her appearance.

When she was little, Evie was drawn to a statue of the Sacred Heart of Jesus. In her child's mind, he was like her—different from everybody else because his heart was on the outside. She thought that Jesus must have felt the same kind of loneliness that she did. In her innocence, Evie struck up a friendship with Jesus.

As a teenager, Evie suffered from deep insecurities and struggled with an eating disorder. In adulthood, she had trouble making friends and never dated. She went to counseling and tried to overcome the intense feelings of shame and self-hatred that bubbled inside her, but she seemed to make little progress.

Still Evie clung to her faith and a relationship with Jesus and the Sacred Heart. She was drawn to a special celebration at her church, to celebrate the Solemnity of the Sacred Heart. The Mass was sparsely attended, so Evie sat right before the altar. In front of her was a large statue of the Sacred Heart that reminded her of the one from her childhood.

After Mass was over, the priest and deacon proceeded to process the statue. Because there were so few people, they stopped before each Mass goer for a prolonged period of time, praying as they did. When they came to Evie, she began to cry. An incredible wave of love rushed through her, such as she had never felt before. She heard a voice in the distance (was it the priest's?) soothingly saying over and over again, "Evie, you are loved so very, very much!"

Long after the statue moved on, Evie continued to experience a sense of awe mixed with relief and joy. She felt that a huge burden had been lifted from her. Within the depth of her being, she felt loved and loveable. The Sacred Heart had broken through.

Evie said, "In my mind and heart, I was always that shy little girl in the shadows who nobody liked. Jesus showed me the person that he saw, and it changed my whole life."

♥ *Heart Note* ♥

Reflect upon the ways in which you have experienced comfort in your life. How have you offered comfort to others? Is there a way that Jesus can comfort you now?

Promise Three in Scripture

Many are the afflictions of the righteous,
> but the Lord rescues them from them all. (Psalm 34:19)

For a brief moment I abandoned you,
> but with great compassion I will gather you. (Isaiah 54:7)

Do not be afraid, little flock, for it is your Father's good pleasure to give you the kingdom. (Luke 12:32)

Very truly, I tell you, if you ask anything of the Father in my name, he will give it to you. (John 16:33)

Heart of Jesus, save us now!

Chapter Fifteen

A Promise of Refuge

I will be their refuge in life and especially in death.

W e all fear death. It's natural to cling to life, and no matter how much faith a person may have, what lies beyond remains a mystery. But St. Margaret Mary was adamant regarding this fourth promise:

> I have found no remedy more efficacious in all my troubles than the Sacred Heart. In it I repose without anxiety. The sick and sinners will find in it a secure place of refuge. This divine and loving Heart is my hope and my refuge; its merits are my salvation, my life and my resurrection.[1]

HEALING STORIES

Ernest and Grace had their home enthroned with the assistance of their daughter Gloria, a worldwide promoter of enthronements to the Sacred Heart. Ernest was not a churchgoing man, but he honored the ministry of his daughter. He was very proud of the work that she did for the Sacred Heart, even if he didn't fully understand it.

Ernest participated in the enthronement with Grace, Gloria, and other family members. Before the hanging of the image above the kitchen table, Ernest kissed it. His daughter had never seen a man do that before at an enthronement, nor has she witnessed it since. It was the only outward expression of reverence or devotion that Ernest had ever made.

One day, Gloria was hosting the traveling image of Our Lady of Guadalupe at the Sacred Heart Center, the headquarters of the Sacred Heart Apostolate in Syracuse, New York. Some two hundred visitors streamed through the doors. The next step was to take the image to the sidewalk in front of the local Planned Parenthood for a prayer vigil. As the group started to leave, Gloria was informed that her father had just died from a massive heart attack. He had been seated at the kitchen table, directly under the image of the Sacred Heart.

Gloria could only say, "It's OK, because Our Lady is here!" But as the group drove in a solemn caravan to Planned Parenthood, reality sunk in, and Gloria began to weep.

On arriving at the prayer vigil site, a priest and other people approached to offer their condolences to Gloria. Word had spread among the crowd of Ernest's passing. Special prayers were said, and Gloria was assured that prayers for Ernest would be said at every church that the pilgrim image of Our Lady visited. This brought tremendous comfort to her.

Even though Ernest had never been to church and was not even Catholic, fourteen priests were present at his burial! This is when Gloria realized the true meaning of the promise, "I will be their refuge in life and especially in death." But that is not the end of the story!

Grace lived many years after Ernest's death, to the age of ninety-five. During that time, she watched many friends die and was always hit hard by their passing. It was clear to Gloria that her mother was very fearful of death. Even though Grace was deeply devoted to the Blessed Mother and her home was still enthroned to the Sacred Heart, she clearly did not want to die.

When Grace was suffering with terminal cancer and coming close to her final hour, she went into the hospital. For many days she refused to close her eyes because she was afraid of dying. Her children and her grandchildren stood vigil in an effort to calm her and accompany her in her suffering, both physical and spiritual.

Gloria left a little booklet by a contemporary visionary in the hospital room. It described what death and heaven were like. Gloria hoped to comfort the grandchildren and put them more at ease with the loss of their beloved grandmother. Instead, Gloria's son read a passage aloud to Grace, who by this time was very near death and comatose. After reading the words that described how Jesus and loved ones are there to greet those who die, Grace opened her eyes and, with tears streaming down her cheeks, smiled and took her last breath peacefully, just as Jesus promised.

* * *

Katie lived a hard but very interesting life. She was committed to a New York City orphanage in the early 1940s, along with her eight siblings, simply because her parents were deaf. It wasn't easy growing up there. Katie, a somewhat wild spirit, had trouble following the rules. At the age of thirteen, she ran away and joined a traveling burlesque show! From there she became a fairly successful lounge singer.

Katie drifted through life during her twenties and thirties. She tried to reunite with members of her family, with no success. She finally found the love of her life, Harold, at age forty. They settled in upstate New York. Katie experienced eight miscarriages and no live births. For twenty short years, Katie and Harold shared a simple life together. For many of them, Katie took care of Harold, who was much older than Katie and in ill health. When he died, Katie was left to fend for herself once again.

Even though Katie had lived a difficult life, she retained a childlike innocence. She was, in many ways, a very simple soul. As a widow with no children or education, she was also vulnerable, and she lived on the edge of poverty. She retained her street smarts, surviving by her wits and her Catholic faith. She loved Jesus and the Blessed Mother.

Multiple health problems plagued Katie, and eventually she entered intensive care for the last time. In the final stages of congestive heart failure, she seemed very frightened of her impending death. She was immobilized and could not talk because of a ventilator and feeding tube. Even heavy doses of drugs failed to calm her.

Katie's advocates, knowing that she was devoutly Catholic, brought images of the Sacred Heart and the Immaculate Heart of Mary from her home and arranged to have them taped to the ceiling, where Katie could see them. These had an immediate effect. Not only did Katie calm down, but she began folding her hands in prayer and even smiling.

For the next several weeks, Katie didn't stop smiling. One nurse even remarked that it looked as if Katie was glowing! Anytime a nurse or an orderly walked into the room, Katie pointed to the pictures and held up her hands to pray. People would stop and pray with her, at all hours of the day and night. The love of Jesus truly flowed in that room, and there is no doubt that Katie found her final refuge in the embrace of the Sacred Heart.

♥ *Heart Note* ♥

Who might you know who is struggling or suffering? How could you share the Sacred Heart with him or her?

Promise Four in Scripture

The Lord will open for you his rich storehouse, the heavens, to give the rain of your land in its season and to bless all your undertakings. (Deuteronomy 28:12)

Come to me, all you that are weary and are carrying heavy burdens, and I will give you rest. (Matthew 11:28)

Do not let your hearts be troubled. Believe in God, believe also in me. In my Father's house there are many dwelling places. If it were not so, would I have told you that I go to prepare a place for you? And if I go and prepare a place for you, I will come again and will take you to myself, so that where I am, there you may be also. And you know the way to the place where I am going. (John 14:1–4)

Blessed be the God and Father of our Lord Jesus Christ, who has blessed us in Christ with every spiritual blessing in the heavenly places. (Ephesians 1:3)

Sweet Heart of Jesus, be our refuge and our strength!

Chapter Sixteen

A Promise of Abundant Blessings

I will abundantly bless all their undertakings.

A blessing upon all of our undertakings" is a promise that we can take into every area of our lives. Whether we are seeking success at work or school; working hard to maintain our relationships or seeking deeper connection with Jesus on a spiritual level, he is ready, willing and able to assist us in all of our affairs.

St. Margaret Mary offers this blessing to us: "May the Sacred Heart accomplish in you all his designs and be himself your strength and your stay, so as to enable you to bear courageously the weight of your responsibility."[1]

I know of one mother who has embraced this promise since her children were young, still sends them off to school each morning by making the sign of the cross on their foreheads with holy water and reminding them that Jesus will bless them in all that they do if they do it out of love for his Sacred Heart. You would think that middle-school aged children might protest such a ritual, but they are quick to remind her, if she forgets!

HEALING STORIES

Life can certainly throw us some curve balls, and one of the evil one's tactics is to keep us dodging them to the point of despair. This could have been the story for one man, the head of a company that was facing bankruptcy. The day that he could not make payroll happened to be the day when he had scheduled an Enthronement of the Sacred Heart at his place of business.

This humble owner of the company began the procession through the building with the image of the Sacred Heart. As he approached the boardroom, where the image was to be displayed, his secretary came up to him and announced an important phone call. He told her to take a message, but she insisted that this was a phone call he would want to take, so he did. The person on the line was in the process of writing a $700,000 check to the company, which would cover the payroll cost and then some!

That is only the beginning of the story. The company steered clear of bankruptcy but still struggled somewhat. The man decided to move the Sacred Heart image from the boardroom to the hall just inside the entrance way. There, everyone who entered the building—workers and customers alike—could see Jesus. Not only did business pick up, but the boss noticed a distinct improvement in morale.

Many workers would stop briefly at the image before starting their shift. Some would gently touch the portrait on their way home to their families. The owner could see changes in the hearts of his employees and a softening of attitude among those who walked through the doors of his company. He prayed daily that those changes might carry over into his employees' and customers' families and homes.

The Lord's promise to "bless abundantly" came in many ways to the company and the lives of those who worked there. Today the business is thriving, enjoying not only financial success but also success in the things that truly matter to the Sacred Heart of Jesus.

* * *

Father Brennan Joseph is a Conventual Franciscan friar and an associate pastor of an inner-city parish where I live. The parish is located in an area where there is a mixture of poverty and promise. The large church is a pastoral hub for the many refugees who have settled in the community. It serves as a means of material provision, through a food pantry and medical ministry, for those who struggle economically.

Fr. Brennan's order has moved him from place to place because of his ability to deal with difficult people and situations. Any success that he has had in his thirty years of ministry, he attributes to the Sacred Heart. Father was eager to relate how the Sacred Heart has blessed him and his undertakings.

In my childhood home, at the top of the staircase, was a big picture of the Sacred Heart. As a little kid, I would often go and talk to him and ask him for help. I love theater, and I had plans to go to college for drama, but he had better plans. He led me to religious life.

For me, the Sacred Heart devotion is a very simple devotion. I look at him as my friend. The thorns around his heart have always engaged me. As a child, I thought, "You must be in a lot of pain!" As I grew, I would look at the image and realize that my sins make up those thorns. At the same time, I realize that there has not been one thing that I haven't done or been through that the Sacred Heart hasn't carried me through.

I can even look back at the most difficult time of my life and recognize the influence of the Sacred Heart. Before I was ordained, my mother grew ill and died. I was very close to her, and her loss was devastating. I was angry with God and could not believe that he would take my beloved mother from me. One day in the chapel, crying out and begging God for solace, I sensed him speaking to me, saying, "Just trust me."

It wasn't until after I was ordained that I realized that, had my mother lived and needed me in any way, I would have left the seminary to take care of her. This was the way that Jesus preserved my priesthood. His heart has been my greatest love and help.

Even after thirty years of preaching, I still get butterflies before the homily. I have come to accept that this is exactly as it should be, because it is at that time that I am totally dependent on his Sacred Heart. I know in the deepest part of my heart that he gives me the energy and grace to love and serve people, even when they are grumpy or difficult! Through the merits of his Sacred Heart, I am able to be merciful and nonjudgmental and have the compassion of his heart for them.

I know in the marrow of my bones that *he loves me*, and I want people to know that they are *so loved by him*! The day I was ordained, I prayed that every Mass I say and everything I do will let people know how much they are loved. I look at the Sacred Heart, and the love is all there.

You do what you can, and God will do what you can't. In any job, trust in him.

♥ *Heart Note* ♥

Contemplate ways in which you can bring a devotion to the Sacred Heart into every area of your life. Then, keep track of the blessings you receive!

Promise Five in Scripture

God is our refuge and strength,
> a very present help in trouble. (Psalm 46:1)

Come to me, you who desire me,
> and eat your fill of my fruits. (Sirach 24:19)

Let anyone who is thirsty come to me, and let the one who believes in me drink. As the scripture has said, "Out of the believer's heart shall flow rivers of living water." (John 7:37–38)

I came that they may have life, and have it abundantly. (John 10:10)

Holy Heart of Jesus, help me to love you more and more!

Chapter Seventeen

A Promise of Mercy

*Sinners will find in my Heart the source
and infinite ocean of mercy.*

P ope Francis has been speaking about mercy since the very beginning of his papacy. In his homily on March 17, 2013, he said:

> It is not easy to entrust oneself to God's mercy, because it is an abyss beyond our comprehension. But we must!... "Oh, I am a great sinner." "All the better! Go to Jesus: he likes you to tell him these things!" He forgets, he has a very special capacity for forgetting. He forgets, he kisses you, he embraces you and he simply says to you: "Neither do I condemn you; go, and sin no more" (John 8:11).[1]

In March of 2015, Pope Francis announced an Extraordinary Jubilee Year of Mercy, to commence December 8, 2015, the Solemnity of the Immaculate Conception, and close November 20, 2016, the Solemnity of Our Lord Jesus Christ, King of the Universe. He stated, "I am convinced that the whole Church will be able to find in this Jubilee the joy needed to rediscover and make fruitful the mercy of God, with which all of us are called to give consolation to every man and every woman of our time."[2]

These words echo what Jesus told St. Margaret Mary at Paray-le-Monial:

Fear not, it is I Jesus which means Savior. I have come to remind you that the love that fills my heart is a merciful love. I have come for sinners. I am in the Eucharist for sinners. I reveal my heart especially for sinners, that they may all be converted. Sinners will find in my heart a boundless ocean of mercy. Therefore, I ask you to trust me...blindly...with childlike trust.[3]

Mercy is God's love in action and the mission of his heart. Jesus repeated his message of mercy to St. Faustina: "I am Love and Mercy itself." [4]

When we experience God's mercy, it can be a life-changing experience. This next story illustrates how we cannot help but share that mercy with others.

HEALING STORIES

Gloria and Father Bill travel the country conducting parish missions on enthroning the Sacred Heart in homes, parishes, seminaries, and other establishments. On one such mission in Colorado, they were having breakfast in the hotel restaurant. When the waitress came to their table with coffee, she was friendly and outgoing, if not a bit forward. "Good morning, Honey! How are you?" she asked Gloria.

They engaged in a bit more small talk. Then the waitress glanced at Father and asked, "Are you Catholic?" Gloria explained that yes, they were both Catholic, and Father was a Redemptorist priest. She then noticed that the woman's name tag read "Monica." And with Holy Spirit boldness, Gloria asked, "Monica, are *you* Catholic?" The woman grew quiet, evading their gaze, and mumbled something about being a Catholic once but not now.

Gloria looked intently at her watch and proclaimed, "Monica, do you know what time it is? Monica, this is *your* time, this is *your* moment! Now is the time for Fr. Bill to hear your confession! You sit down right here, and I will go to the other side of the restaurant."

The waitress protested that she was not allowed to sit down, so Gloria told her she could lean over and talk to Fr. Bill as if she were taking his order. With that, Gloria left them.

From across the room, Gloria could see Monica bending down to speak to Father as he gently nodded his head, listening intently. Then he raised his hand over her head and uttered the beautiful words of absolution. This was the moment of moments, when in Monica's life heaven opened and mercy poured down. Monica started to cry. When Gloria returned to the table, Monica thanked her profusely and gave her a tight hug.

The next day, Gloria and Fr. Bill went to the same restaurant. Monica was there, but she looked different. She made sure to wait on them again so she could relate a miracle of mercy that had transpired the night before. She explained that since her confession, she had never felt so much peace. In fact, she was so filled with joy that she had not wanted to go to sleep the night before, for fear that the feeling would go away!

Late that night, she had received a phone call from her father, whom she hadn't heard from in many years. He simply blurted out, "Monica, this is your father, and I called to ask you to forgive me!"

Monica was taken aback at these words from her estranged father. Old hurt feelings surfaced, and she hesitated. Then she remembered how much peace she had experienced when she was touched by God's mercy and love, when she had asked forgiveness for herself. Her heart was flooded with a desire for her father to feel the exact same relief and joy, and she said from the bottom of her heart, "Dad, I forgive you."

* * *

The story of the Samaritan woman is the longest recorded

conversation that Jesus has with anyone in Scripture (see John 4). She is a lonely woman who is burdened with shame because of her lifestyle. She draws water by herself at midday, an indication that she has been shunned by the townsfolk because of her numerous husbands. She is living with a man who is not her husband.

It's not hard to relate to this woman. She, in some ways, represents all of us at one time or another in our lives. The fact is that we all need God's mercy, all of the time!

So what happens when the Samaritan woman encounters Jesus? At first the woman is startled, confused, and a little bit defensive. A woman did not talk with a man in public, especially a Samaritan with a Jew, and yet here was Jesus initiating conversation! (He starts the conversation with us too; we just have to listen carefully.)

Jesus says something like this to the woman: If you only knew the gift that God wants to give you, you would ask for that and never be thirsty again. You would never go unfulfilled but drink of living water that will satisfy forever! And the woman responds, "Sir, give me this water, so that I may never be thirsty or have to keep coming here to draw water" (John 4:15).

Jesus wants more for her though. He wants her to be completely free and receive the fullness of his mercy. So in his presence she finds the courage to "come clean" and reveal the painful truth of her past and her present. Maybe this is her first confession. Something about Jesus makes it safe for her to be who she really is. He in turn heals her of her shame.

When we embrace devotion to the Sacred Heart, the same kind of transformation can happen! Our broken hearts can be healed, and our shame can be conquered. Joannie's story is a beautiful example of this.

* * *

Joannie was a retired schoolteacher who wanted to have an enthrone-ment in her home. She did not have anyone to attend the ceremony, but this did not stop her. Through her work at a local food pantry, she often met people who were down-and-out, and who needed to expe-rience the love of his Sacred Heart. So she committed the matter to prayer, and God answered that prayer in a remarkable way!

When the day came for the enthronement, she informed the facil-itator that three people would attend. Her three guests included a woman in her thirties, a man named Pedro, also in his thirties, and another woman around fifty.

When the image of the Sacred Heart was brought in, Joannie held it before the younger woman for a long time. She then quietly asked, "Look into his eyes; what do you see?" The woman began to cry. Joannie asked the same of Pedro, who also began to weep. The older woman looked much tougher. When Joannie approached her with the same question, the woman's body language softened noticeably.

After the enthronement, as the guests gathered for refreshments, they shared their stories. The woman in her fifties pulled up her sleeve and revealed track marks where she had shot heroin. She admitted she was a prostitute. "When I looked at Jesus, it was like a shell fell off of me," she said.

The younger woman had been sexually abused. She said that she felt pure love for the first time when she looked into Jesus's eyes.

Pedro was an alcoholic. When he looked at Jesus, he realized a void in his heart that he was trying to fill with alcohol. As he went through the ceremony, he felt Jesus filling that void.

Joannie was indeed a special soul who always attracted those in need. She took Jesus at his word: He promised that sinners would find an infinite ocean of his mercy. And lifelong healings began at her house that day.

♥ *Heart Note* ♥

What does the word *mercy* mean to you? Journal your thoughts. When have you needed mercy and when have you extended it?

PROMISE SIX IN SCRIPTURE

Though your sins are like scarlet,
  they shall be like snow;
though they are red like crimson,
  they shall become like wool.
If you are willing and obedient,
  you shall eat the good of the land. (Isaiah 1:18–19)

Go and learn what this means, "I desire mercy, not sacrifice." For I have come to call not the righteous but sinners. (Matthew 9:13)

Everything that the Father gives me will come to me, and anyone who comes to me I will never drive away. (John 6:37)

Sacred Heart of Jesus, pour your mercy upon us.

Chapter Eighteen

A Promise of Fervent Faith

Lukewarm souls shall become fervent.

In the book of Revelation, God warns those who are lukewarm, "I know your works; you are neither cold nor hot. I wish that you were either cold or hot. So, because you are lukewarm…I am about to spit you out of my mouth" (Revelation 3:15–16).

This is proof that God wants us to live our lives fully engaged and fully alive. Straddling the middle way is not Christ-like. As we learn more about the Heart of Jesus, it is impossible to remain casual about and unaffected by his immeasurable love.

We grow lukewarm for lots of reasons. Sin, of course, is the greatest barrier to having a fervent, on-fire soul. The power of love is diminished in us when we turn away from Love, not just in the big ways but in all the little ways as well.

We may be tempted to dismiss our transgressions, but they bog us down and dim our souls. They chip away at our consciences and create confusion and doubt. Satan is fully satisfied when we live our lives halfway, when we conduct ourselves in a lackadaisical and presumptive way. Perhaps we count on Jesus to forgive us even when we neglect to confess what we have done wrong or fail to believe that what we are doing (or not doing) is sinful in the first place.

St. Margaret Mary put it this way:

> You know that there is no middle course, and it is a question of
> being saved or lost. It depends on us: either we may choose to

love God eternally with the Saints in heaven…or else renounce their happiness by giving to nature all for which it craves.[1]

The bottom line is that true love is never lukewarm. Jesus wants more for us. He wants to enflame our hearts with the fire of his love and a desire for heaven.

The Sacred Heart devotion is the surest means to receive the gift of fervency from Jesus. He wants to establish the kingdom of his love through *our* hearts. In this regard, St. Margaret Mary again offers good counsel:

> Our Lord loves you and wishes to see you advance with great speed in the way of His love…. Therefore do not bargain with Him, but give Him all, and you will find all in His divine Heart.[2]

HEALING STORIES

Even hearts that have been devoted to Jesus for a long time can grow lukewarm. I know this to be true from my own life.

I love Jesus very much and have been deeply engaged with my faith, even writing and speaking for the Lord. Yet for several years, I struggled with dryness and a sense of routine in my prayer life. I felt somewhat cut off from my emotions and weary in nearly every aspect of my life. Over time, my standards slipped in my interactions with others at my job. It became easy for me to do what everyone else did rather than do the right thing.

That's when the Lord led me to confession and to a crossroads. After much angst and indecision, fear and wrestling, I decided to leave my career, take a year off, and try to discern what direction he wanted me to go in next. After I gave my notice to my employer, the fog and heaviness I had been carrying around cleared up rather quickly.

Almost immediately, and through a number of divinely ordained circumstances, I became involved in the Sacred Heart Apostolate—a global movement and ministry based in my hometown of Syracuse, New York. I was swept up in the activities and the blessings that accompany anyone who endeavors to promote the Sacred Heart of Jesus in the world. While I have been involved in many efforts previously, nothing has grabbed a hold of my heart and freed me from my own self more than this work for the Sacred Heart. It is as if the Lord opened a door to a tiny corner of heaven in my soul.

Now I can say that my heart rests firmly in the heart of Jesus through Mary. My relationship with Jesus has changed: It has grown in intimacy, in a way that is difficult to put into words. He has taken up residence in my heart, and now we go through everything together. It's all for him and not for me.

Jesus can take restless, wavering souls like mine and turn them into mighty minions in the empire of his love. All of us can recover a sense of the richness of his love. All of us can grow in love, forgive, and offer mercy through the devotion of the Sacred Heart. God has a plan; we just need to cooperate with it, trust in his mercy, and get out of the way—letting him carry it out!

* * *

Brandon, the father of two young boys, looked like the perfect family man. He was devoted to his wife, Lisa, and actively participated in the boys' lives, following their sports and trying to be the best role model he could. Yet there was certain and troubling emotional distance between Brandon and his family, which he attributed to his past. A very difficult relationship with his own father yielded feelings of inadequacy.

Brandon's childhood had been chaotic and marked by abuse.

When he was thirteen, his father left the family for good. Brandon never told anyone, but something in his heart died that day. His sense of alienation caused him to be guarded and suspicious. He never experienced the warmth, security, love, and acceptance that a family is supposed to provide. Now he struggled to create that for his own children.

Lisa and Brandon learned about devotion to the Sacred Heart through the Legion of Mary. The founder of the legion, Frank Duff, had a fervent devotion to the Sacred Heart and made enthronements of the Sacred Heart a part of the legion's mission and work. Lisa brought an image of the Sacred Heart home and began praying especially for an increased sense of love and closeness within her family. Brandon secretly prayed that his feelings of inadequacy and emotional distance would dissipate.

One day, after several months of praying, Brandon was attending Sunday Mass with his family when he experienced something that he will never forget. Sitting quietly in the pew after receiving Communion, Brandon was struck with an interior image. It was as if he was looking at himself as a child, playing in his childhood home, but instead of his own family surrounding him, he saw the Blessed Mother, Jesus, and St. Joseph. The image brought him an incredible sense of peace and love. He also received a very simple message from Jesus: "Family is good, and you will forever be a part of mine."

After that encounter, the hesitations, insecurities, and sense of alienation that Brandon had been carrying around with him were wiped away. Jesus replaced his lukewarm and tentative heart with a father's heart that was free to love and trust and truly enjoy the firm roots that God created family to provide.

♥ *Heart Note* ♥

In what areas of your life have you become lukewarm? Write a prayer, inviting the Holy Spirit and Sacred Heart of Jesus to "stir into flame" a strong desire to grow in these areas.

PROMISE SEVEN IN SCRIPTURE

A new heart I will give you, and a new spirit I will put within you; and I will remove from your body the heart of stone and give you a heart of flesh. (Ezekiel 36:26)

I came to bring fire to the earth, and how I wish it were already kindled! (Luke 12:49)

Hope does not disappoint us, because God's love has been poured into our hearts through the Holy Spirit that has been given to us. (Romans 5:5)

Sacred Heart of Jesus, inflame us with your love.

Chapter Nineteen

A Promise of Perfection

Fervent souls shall quickly mount to high perfection.

Why is it important for our souls to be perfect? As faulty human beings, dogged by original sin, are we capable of perfection? Isn't perfection just for the saints?

These are valid questions. Jesus answers them all with his heart. Holiness is an attainable goal for each one of us because Jesus makes it possible.

St. Claude de la Colombière was known in his time as a brilliant teacher, preacher, and director of souls. His counsel is simple and straightforward:

> As perfection consists in trying to please God in everything and to please Him only, we must not hesitate when we get an opportunity of pleasing Him…. It is God only who can sanctify us… for of ourselves we have neither sufficient light nor strength.[1]
>
> God must do everything. All the better; there will be no fear of failure. We have only to acknowledge our powerlessness and to be fervent and constant in asking for help through the intercession of Mary, to whom God refuses nothing…. [2]

St. Margaret Mary clearly stated the means to perfection: "Nothing unites us so closely to the Sacred Heart of Jesus as the cross, which is the most precious pledge of His love."[3] Our crosses, burdens, and trials are what lead us down the path of holiness. When we seek and apply the graces that we need to endure our crosses, we put our faith in action.

It is important to remember that this is a matter of faith and not of feeling. We may *feel* broken, sorrowful, or intensely distracted by our sufferings. We may even feel angry, impatient, or hopeless at times. In other words, we don't have to feel holy or look holy on the outside to ensure that we are indeed on the road to holiness. When we persevere in faith, without feeling like it, we progress along the path to perfection more than we think.

Again, St. Margaret Mary offers a suggestion: "I think He intends to try you like gold in the crucible, so as to number you among His most faithful servants. Therefore, you must lovingly embrace all occasions of suffering, considering them as precious tokens of His love."[4] We can ask for the grace to receive our crosses and sufferings with love, seeing them as a way that Jesus uses to draw us nearer to him and make us holier. Then those pains take on a new dimension.

Truly, the world's view of perfection is not God's. The quiet lady in the back pew at church, the bank clerk who cashes our paychecks, the young seminarian, the traffic cop, you and I—we are all on the road to perfection. With Jesus in the driver's seat, we will get to our destination! This is his promise if we consent to enter the territory of his heart.

* * *

Catherine was a woman after God's own heart. She discovered the Sacred Heart devotion as a housewife and mother during the 1970s and immediately had her home enthroned. She also began promoting home enthronements in her diocese, to share her zeal and love for Jesus and offer hope to others. Little did she know how vital these actions would become in her life.

As her children grew, challenges in her home became more formidable. Her daughter Emily, always a risk taker, fell in with the wrong crowd and became involved with drugs. Catherine clung to the promises of Jesus and his Sacred Heart. She prayed in earnest for freedom from addiction for her daughter.

Months of prayers turned into years and then decades. Countless false starts and failed hopes, repeated brushes with the law, empty promises from Emily, second chances, attempts at rehabilitation—all fell short. Through it all, Catherine continued to go before Jesus, pleading with a mother's broken heart on behalf of her daughter.

One day, Catherine's prayers were answered. After hitting rock bottom, Emily became clean and sober. Eventually, she found her way back to the Catholic faith, as did the man who had introduced her to and supplied her with drugs all those years!

Catherine was overjoyed. She was grateful to Jesus and his Sacred Heart for his incredible faithfulness. He had given her the strength to persevere in prayer, and now this miracle of mercy had changed the course of her daughter's life and heart.

Then, Emily presented an outrageous request of her mother: She wanted to bring the former drug dealer into Catherine's home for dinner. Emily wanted her mother to open her home and her heart to the man who had brought much darkness, destruction, and despair to their lives. Within this request was an invitation by Jesus for Catherine to forgive.

As with any opportunity of grace, there is a moment of truth. Catherine had spent a majority of her adult life promoting the love and mercy of Jesus in his Sacred Heart; now it was time for her to *live* that message in the most profound way, and she felt she could not do it. Her heart was so cold toward this man that she could barely stand to think of him, let alone allow him into her presence.

But Jesus reminded Catherine that it wasn't into *her* presence that the man was coming but into his own. When we enthrone the Sacred Heart of Jesus in our homes, he lives there in our midst. His presence is alive and active, and he remains with us always. He greets and meets all who come into our homes, whether they are aware of it or not.

Still, Catherine was hesitant. She was afraid of how she and her husband might respond to this man. When the day for the dinner came, Catherine prayed and prayed.

As the door opened and the man walked over the threshold, smiling and holding Emily's hand, Catherine could not breathe. Suddenly, and quite unexpectedly, she was seized by an overwhelming sense of love. She felt her heart pounding hard as it seemed to expand in her chest to contain the intense compassion and love she felt for the man standing before her. It was as if the Lord was pouring his mercy into her very being. The memories and pain of years—the bitterness, resentment, and fear—were washed away in that moment. Catherine knew in that instant that she was experiencing the love that Jesus had for this man. Jesus was giving her a heart transplant right there in her living room!

Catherine was so overcome that she had to leave the room. She fled to her bedroom, where she fell on her knees in prayer to the Lord. After a time, Emily knocked on her mother's door and asked, "Mom, are you OK? What happened in there?"

Catherine responded, "I think I just had a Sacred Heart attack!"

* * *

St. Mother Teresa said that "pain, sorrow and suffering are but the kiss of Jesus—a sign that you have come so close to Him that He can kiss you."[5] The following story is a poignant illustration of these beautiful words.

During the course of a Sacred Heart Mission, people are invited to venerate a crucifix. It is an invitation to contemplate Our Lord's suffering and to ask him for help with our own. First, families with small children are invited to come up. In watching them, it's easy to tell which youngsters have never been that close to a crucifix, because they take a few extra seconds to look upon the twisted figure on the cross.

On one particular evening, two young boys approached the crucifix with their mother. One boy was blind, and the other was in a wheelchair, with some very obvious and significant physical challenges. Very gently, the mother spoke to her blind son. She carefully placed his hand over the nail piercing Jesus's foot. The boy touched the nail, then pulled his hand back for a moment, only to return his tiny fingers to lightly rub Jesus's feet.

Slowly, the mother guided her little boy's hand to Jesus's pierced side. As he felt the wound there, the boy again drew back, as if he could feel the pain of it himself. Then he returned to the corpus, moving to caress Jesus's face and then the crown of thorns. These few moments seemed to last a long time, and many who observed the encounter were left with tears in their eyes.

Next, the child in the wheelchair spoke quietly with his mother. It was clear that he could not pick his head up to see the crucifix. So the teenagers whose task it was to hold it brought the crucifix to the boy and rested it in his lap. With great effort, the boy managed to contemplate our Lord in his suffering.

These two young boys remind us that we do not have to be perfect as the world defines it to be perfectly united to the heart of Jesus. We meet him at the cross. We love him and tend to his wounds even more because of our own.

♥ *Heart Note* ♥

What are your thoughts, fears, and beliefs about suffering? How would they change if you were to consider suffering as a token of Christ's love?

Promise Eight in Scripture

I walk in the way of righteousness,
  along the paths of justice,
endowing with wealth those who love me,
  and filling their treasuries. (Proverbs 8:20–21)

I give thanks to my God always for you because of the grace of God that has been given you in Christ Jesus, for in every way you have been enriched in him, in speech and knowledge of every kind. (1 Corinthians 1:4–5)

I pray that you may have the power to comprehend, with all the saints, what is the breadth and length and height and depth, and to know the love of Christ that surpasses knowledge, so that you may be filled with all the fullness of God. (Ephesians 3:18–19)

I am confident of this, that the one who began a good work among you will bring it to completion by the day of Jesus Christ. (Philippians 1:6)

O sweet Jesus, meek and humble of heart, make our hearts like unto thine.

Chapter Twenty

A Promise of Faithfulness

I will bless every place in which an image of my Heart is
exposed and honored.

Most people who have known about Sacred Heart devotion associate it with the image that hung in their home or in their grandparents' home when they were young. In fact, nearly every Catholic home in the 1940s and 1950s had the picture prominently displayed. This was largely due to the ninth promise.

The Enthronement of the Sacred Heart is a fulfillment of Jesus's promise to be with us "always, to the end of the age" (Matthew 28:20). Countless stories speak to the faithfulness of God to those who have placed the image in a prominent place in their homes, businesses, schools, and churches. The Lord's blessings, big and small, abound in the lives of those who claim this promise.

> Jesus said, "I will reign through my Heart," and the Enthronement is the official and social recognition of the sovereignty of the Sacred Heart of Jesus over the Christian family....
> [It also serves to] re-establish the rule of Christ over nations....[1]

Placing the image in a ceremonial manner is just the first step. The image itself reminds us of the true desire of Jesus to be present and central in our lives, because his presence will make us the happiest possible in this life and prepare us for the next.

Fr. Mateo's two spiritual mottos for the enthronement movement are "Thy kingdom come!" and "He must reign." The worthy goals of enthronement are:

- revitalization of faith and love in the home
- reconciliation and forgiveness among family members, through contemplation of the Heart of Jesus
- reconnecting the family with the parish, to inspire a "family to family" evangelization
- strong family witness of God's plan for marriage and family
- greater reverence for the Eucharist
- greater appreciation for the Word of God
- a more intimate relationship with Jesus and each other
- renewed and loving awareness and embrace of the truths of the Catholic faith

HEALING STORIES

Tom and Mary Kay were married on Thanksgiving Day, and their first child, Christopher, was born less than two years later. The couple looked forward to having another child, and it was a mystery to them when Mary Kay did not conceive. They were concerned enough to have a medical examination, but the doctor found nothing that would prevent conception.

Shortly after the exam, Tom and Kay heard a presentation by the West Coast director of the Apostolate of Prayer, promoting enthronement of the Sacred Heart. They learned that there were great favors bestowed on individuals who honored Christ in their homes and made a covenant of love with the Sacred Heart. So on the Feast of the Transfiguration, Tom and Kay enthroned the Sacred Heart in their hearts and home in the presence of Christopher and a few close friends. Together they claimed the promise of Jesus, "I will bless every dwelling in which an image of my heart is both exposed and honored."

Our Lord was faithful to his promise. Nine months and eight days later, Tom and Kay welcomed their second son, Paul Gerard.

* * *

"I go to him for *everything!*" Those are the words of a very proud father of six. "When my kids see me sitting before the image [of the Sacred Heart], they know that I am talking to Jesus." His wife agrees that "having Jesus enthroned in our home is the best thing our family has ever done."

These parents, Bill and Samantha, make it a point to pray together whenever possible. They bring to the Lord every household decision. They encourage their six teens and preteens to do the same.

For instance, one of the high school boys couldn't find a summer job. Samantha suggested that once a day he sit with Jesus (as Dad does) and say a decade of the rosary. She urged her son to honor the Blessed Mother in this way and see what happened. One of the boy's brothers piped up, "If you are really serious about that job, you would say a whole rosary!" So the young man did, and within two days, he had a job!

Bill and Samantha share that things don't always work out that way. They teach their children that it is "not the results of our prayer that are important but that we pray with trust and confidence in the promises that Jesus gave us." The important witness of these parents mirrors for their children the trust relationship with Jesus that they so vitally need to succeed both materially and spiritually in the world.

"We get all our help from Jesus," Bill says. "He is the head of this household."

* * *

Nowadays, many things threaten to usurp the authority and primacy of Jesus in our lives. Enthronement of his Sacred Heart provides a necessary juxtaposition to the tyranny of modernism, moral relativism, and the godlessness of societies. Fr. Mateo referred to Jesus as the "King of Love." Surely we need Jesus to establish his reign in our homes, families, and beyond.

"The Enthronement of Jesus means dethronement of Satan."[2] We don't have to look far to get a glimpse of the reign that Satan has over our world and in our homes. We have become confused as to where our allegiances lie. Satan breeds this confusion and the world's contempt for all things holy. He is the father of lies.

Through the enthronement of Jesus, we proclaim the truth. Pope Pius XI said in his encyclical establishing the Feast of Christ the King:

> Oh, what happiness would be ours if all men, individuals, families, and nations, would but let themselves be governed by Christ! "Then at length," to use the words of Pope Leo XIII, "will many evils be cured; then will the law regain its former authority; peace with all its blessings be restored. Men will sheathe their swords and lay down their arms when all freely acknowledge and obey the authority of Christ, and every tongue confesses that the Lord Jesus Christ is in the glory of God the Father."[3]

Truly, this devotion is transformational, and not just on the heart level. It has the potential to change the tide of our culture—away from the false gods that threaten to destroy it and on toward the triumph of love.

* * *

Sometimes we don't even know what are the problems that need Jesus's remedy, but he knows.

Jake and Tina were "good Catholics" who were active in parish life and trying their best to live out their faith. Nevertheless, Jake felt that "the world won out" as far as his young adult children were concerned. Even though both his daughter and son had gone to Catholic schools, neither was practicing the faith. His daughter, in particular, had said she "would never go back!"

Jake and Tina could see how this lack of connection to her faith impacted their daughter. She seemed to have no real direction in life and, though living at home, no connection with the family.

Jake and Tina felt that a home enthronement of the Sacred Heart could make a difference in the lives of their children. It could help the family "weather the storm" of cultural influence that was chipping away at their foundation of faith and stealing their joy.

When the day came for the enthronement, the daughter and son participated reluctantly. Jake noted that it was a beautiful and powerful experience, the first faith-based event since the children were small. Jake sensed a presence and a calm, to which he clung after the ceremony. Never could he have known how much he would need to hold on to that presence and the promise of Jesus's Sacred Heart.

Several days after the enthronement, a beloved family friend died suddenly. This tragic event sent the entire family into a tailspin, but it was especially hard for the daughter. She seemed to be beside herself in grief. One night, it became clear that she was not OK mentally or physically. It was found that she was dealing with a serious addiction, of which the parents were not even aware.

The daughter was placed in treatment, and both Jake and Tina were left wondering where the promises of peace and joy of the enthronement had gone! In fact, Tina was angry at God. Then someone in the family pointed out that at times, the Sacred Heart has to *clean house* before he can establish his reign within it.

In fact, this is exactly what was happening. Jesus did not take away all of the problems for this family, but instead he shed his light on problems so that they could be healed. Even though there was no evidence of peace, Jake and Tina prayed their prayer of renewal to the Sacred Heart every day and prayed for their daughter and son.

When their daughter returned from rehab, there was a definite change in her. She talked about her faith and thanked God. Eventually, she went back to church.

At the time of this writing, things are not perfect for this family, but they are stronger and more hopeful than they have ever been. Jake, in telling this story, is quick to point out that, even though it seemed as if "all hell broke loose" in the family after the enthronement, this was exactly what the family needed. Their brokenness came out of the darkness and into the flow of mercy that gushes forth from the wound in Jesus's Sacred Heart. They are still reeling but also *resting* in the promises of his Sacred Heart.

Jake says, "You have nothing to fear! The Sacred Heart is how we can reclaim our kids for Christ." His is a powerful witness of what devotion to the Sacred Heart can do for even those hurts of which we are not yet aware in our lives.

Fr. Mateo's vision was to conquer the whole world for the heart of Jesus, home after home, family after family. All that is disordered is reordered in the heart of Jesus. Through enthronement, Jesus protects, provides, and preserves what rightly belongs to him—our families and our souls.

♥ *Heart Note* ♥

Contemplate what or whom must be dethroned in order to establish Jesus as the King of your heart. Ponder the words of Jesus when he was asked about his kingship:

Pilate asked him, "So you are a king?" Jesus answered, "You say that I am a king. For this I was born, and for this I came into the world, to testify to the truth. Everyone who belongs to the truth listens to my voice." (John 18:37)

Promise Nine in Scripture

Moses made a serpent of bronze, and put it upon a pole; and whenever a serpent bit someone, that person would look at the serpent of bronze and live. (Numbers 21:9)

Just as Moses lifted up the serpent in the wilderness, so must the Son of Man be lifted up, that whoever believes in him may have eternal life. (John 3:14–15)

They will look on the one whom they have pierced. (John 19:37)

Sacred Heart of Jesus, we adore you, and we praise you.

Chapter Twenty-One

A Priestly Promise

I will give to priests the power to touch
the most hardened hearts.

Priests are entrusted with the supreme gift and sacred responsibility of consecrating bread and wine into the Body and Blood of Jesus. They act *in persona Christi* (in the person of Christ) during the celebration of the Mass and as *alter Christus* (another Christ) here on earth. This profound calling is realized through the sacrament of holy orders.

Priests share in the universal dimensions of the mission that Christ entrusted to the apostles. The spiritual gift they have received in ordination prepares them, not for a limited and restricted mission, "but for the fullest, in fact the universal mission of salvation 'to the end of the earth,'" "prepared in spirit to preach the Gospel everywhere" (*CCC*, 1565).[1]

Pope Benedict XVI, beginning the Year of Priests on the Solemnity of the Sacred Heart in 2009, stated:

> The priest is a servant of Christ, in the sense that his existence, configured to Christ...acquires an essentially relational character: he is *in* Christ, *for* Christ and *with* Christ, at the service of humankind. Because he belongs to Christ, the priest is radically at the service of all people: he is the minister of their salvation, their happiness and their authentic liberation, developing,

in this gradual assumption of Christ's will, in prayer, in "being heart to heart" with him....[2]

St. John Vianney, the holy Curé of Ars and patron saint of priests, said, "If we really understood the priest on earth, we would die not of fright, but of love.... The Priesthood is the love of the heart of Jesus" (*CCC*, 1589).[3]

Is it any wonder that, with such a tremendous and awesome mission, the priesthood is under attack from all sides? They labor for souls in dangerous and difficult circumstances and face all manner of persecution. In many countries, they are martyred for their faith.

In the West, there has been a shortage of men answering the call to the priesthood. The so-called crisis in vocations is not because the Holy Spirit has stopped inspiring but because many young men, immersed in the world, are oblivious to the call or have not had the soil of their hearts tended to receive it.

It is no coincidence that, of the ten priests that I interviewed for this book, all grew up in homes where devotion to the Sacred Heart was part of their everyday lives. Each one of them indicated that the seed of his vocation was nourished by the Sacred Heart. Holy priests come from holy families, where the members recognize themselves as the domestic church. In fact, the family is the "first seminary," where virtues, sacrifice, prayer, and a love of Jesus and the Catholic faith are modeled and cultivated. Families are sacred, with their own dignity and their responsibility to raise saints.

HEALING STORIES

Michael is a twenty-one-year-old seminarian who speaks thoughtfully about his decision to leave college, a promising career, and his girlfriend of three years to enter the seminary. He contemplated the love of the Sacred Heart during his decision-making and experienced a great solidarity with the Sacred Heart. He explained:

There is suffering, but there is love and His Heart that made the supreme sacrifice for me.... Through it there is total redemption and complete love. It is a great paradox that the key to my happiness comes through the horrific murder of God. His Sacred Heart is where all grace comes from, and when you know that God is with you and cares about you, it makes all the difference in the world!

Michael wrote about a moving experience he had with the Sacred Heart on a blog entitled Seminarian Casual. His post, "My Encounter with the Sacred Heart," is shared here with his joyful permission:

Over Easter break, I volunteered at Fr. Beiting's Appalachian Center in Louisa, Kentucky. It's a journey that has become familiar to me over the years, going down each summer in high school and also last year for spring break. Since it was my sixth time, I didn't think there was going to be anything that would surprise me, but I was wrong.

I had an encounter this year that grabbed hold of my heart more than anything else I've ever experienced in Kentucky. It happened during what's called a "well visit," when volunteers visit local families just to talk to them and spend time with them. I went back to the same home that I went to last year. The family includes a sixth-grader named Sean and his elderly grandmother, who's legally and, as far as I could tell, completely blind.

The group that visited with me were busy talking to the grandmother and another woman who happened to be at the house that day. Sean hunkered down in his room, unwilling to come out and talk. But I knew Sean; I had spent time with him the previous year. So I coerced him out of his room by showing him a picture of us from that visit.

Then we set up a lawn mower that the mission center had been gracious enough to give Sean, to mow his and neighboring lawns. After talking to him about how the mower worked and how to operate it, he started mowing. As I leaned against the wire fence watching him, my heart fell to pieces.

"I bet no one has ever been there for him on a consistent basis," I thought. "I can just tell that he's used to the people who should be loving him walking out on him and never returning, leaving him to do whatever. How could Jesus let this child grow up this way—without parents, without the love and support a child needs?"

As my heart broke for Sean, I realized that I was seeing the Sacred Heart of Jesus at work. I was watching Jesus love precisely in Sean's suffering. Jesus dives into the dark depths of Sean's dysfunctional world to love him. And also in that moment, I understood that God was using me to love Sean. God (for a reason that I'll never understand) used my going to Sean's house and spending time with him as the mechanism to love Sean. And that realization for me was simultaneously awesome and heart wrenching.

It's difficult to go back into that experience with my mind and heart, but in Kentucky this year, I saw the depth of God's love. I saw the suffering Sacred Heart. And even though that hurts, it's important for us to understand just how much God loves us and also the importance of loving others with the Sacred Heart of Christ.[4]

* * *

When we think about hardened hearts, we typically think about people who have strayed into criminal activity or those who openly reject God and all that he stands for. We sometimes miss a more hidden form of hardness. It is the hardness that we harbor toward ourselves. Some of us so relentlessly reject ourselves that we cannot believe in or receive the love that Jesus has for us. Thus we reject him and his mercy outright. This too is hardness of heart.

Certainly there are many people in our culture today who never give a thought to sin. They have no idea that their behavior and choices could lead them to hell. Others focus way too much on their sin; they won't let go of the guilt and shame associated with it. For this latter group, claiming the graces, mercy, and forgiveness of the sacrament of confession is especially difficult.

Father Tom has been a priest for a long time and has spent many long hours in the confessional. Of course, he is never alone there but joined by Jesus, whose image is also present in the form of the Sacred Heart. Throughout his priesthood, Fr. Tom has turned to the Sacred Heart personally for strength, guidance, and solace and has been a quiet promoter of the Sacred Heart, especially from the confessional.

It is there where Father turns many a penitent's attention to the image of our Lord's Sacred Heart. He invites those of contrite yet troubled and burdened hearts to "look at Jesus, looking at you" with nothing but love in his heart. Fr. Tom has seen many a hardened heart melt under that gaze.

Fr. Tom loves to share the story of Fr. Claude de la Colombière's task of testing the authenticity of St. Margaret Mary's visions of the Lord. Fr. Colombière went to confession, then asked Sr. Margaret Mary to have the Lord tell her what sins he had confessed. Some weeks passed. When they met again, the priest asked what the Lord had said. St. Margaret Mary responded, "The Lord said, 'I forgot!'" This response put to rest, once and for all, the question of the authenticity of the visions.

Fr. Tom reminds penitents that if Jesus forgets our transgressions, then so must we. And we must forget the transgressions of others as well. We can throw them into the furnace of his love. Then God can remove our hearts of stone and give us hearts of flesh, just like his Son's.

♥ *Heart Note* ♥

What are your thoughts about confession? Have you been recently?

Ask Jesus to help you make a good confession, with the confidence that he completely forgets and wipes away your sins. If it's been a long time since your last confession, know that things haven't changed much. You start out by praying, "Bless me, Father, for I have sinned. It has been _____ since my last confession. These are my sins." The Lord and the priest will help you from there.

* * *

Father Tariq is a true servant of the Sacred Heart. In 2011, he overcame many obstacles to attend the Sacred Heart World Congress in Paray-le-Monial, France. His intention was to obtain all the information and graces that he would need to bring the devotion of the Sacred Heart back to his home country of Pakistan.

Even though there was risk in carrying it out, his mission was clear: to build a civilization of love and the kingdom of his Sacred Heart in Pakistan. His vision is to eliminate hatred and extremism in Pakistan through the love of the Sacred Heart, the reign of his divine love in every Pakistani's heart and home. While this may sound like a lofty mission, Father makes it clear that it is the mission of Jesus Christ himself, who desires to set every human heart on fire with his love.

Within a year of returning to Pakistan from the World Congress, Fr. Tariq reported remarkable progress:

- Three thousand liturgical calendars were printed in the native language of Urdu, with the image of the Sacred Heart and each month devoted to one of the twelve promises. This was amazing, given Father's limited resources. It was the first liturgical calendar ever made available in Urdu. Through the calendar, people were able to open themselves to the ninth promise, "I will bless the house in which an image of my Sacred Heart is honored and exposed."

- Father and other servants of the Sacred Heart organized a celebration for the Solemnity of the Sacred Heart, which attracted over thirty-five hundred devotees.
- They reached out to ninety-five families, one school, and one convent of the Missionaries of Charity, who prepared families for home enthronements. One of the most grace-filled outcomes of these efforts was that some people preparing for enthronement went to confession for the first time in ten, twenty, forty, or fifty years!

Fr. Tariq and the servants of the Sacred Heart are a small band of souls who take to heart the *big* promises of Jesus for all of those who are devoted to his Sacred Heart.

* * *

The Sacred Heart is an essential shield to protect, preserve, and promote the priesthood today. The Lord has revealed his special desire for priests to promote and live out the devotion through Venerable Mother Louise Margaret Claret de la Touche, a Visitation nun who lived from 1868 to 1915. She wrote a tiny volume entitled *The Sacred Heart and the Priesthood,* which recorded private revelations and light she received regarding the Lord's intentions for priests. The Church has given an imprimatur to her writings.

On the Feast of the Sacred Heart in 1902, the Lord said to Mother Louise Margaret, "My priest is my other self. I love him, but he must be holy. Nineteen centuries ago, twelve men changed the world. They were not merely men but priests. Now once more, twelve men could change the world."[5]

During the series of revelations, which took place over the course of eight days, Jesus gave Mother Louise Margaret a specific mission: to draw all priests to his Sacred Heart.

He said, "I will give you the souls of priests." He also made her aware of an exciting and important fact: that there are aspects of his Sacred Heart that remain unexplored and that have been reserved specifically for priests. "There are dwellings of love in which priests will enter, and where they will find all that they need to be faithful representatives of Jesus."[6]

Through Venerable Mother Louise, Jesus asked for renewed efforts to promulgate devotion to his Sacred Heart in order to combat the evil of the last ages. He wants to renew the world through his Sacred Heart, but he needs his priests to study the devotion and embrace the spirit of love that is behind it. The Lord told Mother Louise:

> I wish to conquer hatred by love. I will send my priests to diffuse love over the earth. I have given them my heart in order that they may see the treasures of love that are in God, that, having drawn for themselves, they may draw for the world. Tell them to go dispense everywhere the treasure of love.[7]

♥ Heart Note ♥

How might you support priests in their devotion to the Sacred Heart?

PROMISE TEN IN SCRIPTURE

> I will give you the keys of the kingdom of heaven, and whatever you bind on earth will be bound in heaven, and whatever you loose on earth will be loosed in heaven. (Matthew 16:19)

Those who are well have no need of a physician, but those who are sick; I have come to call not the righteous but sinners. (Mark 2:17)

Very truly, I tell you, the one who believes in me will also do the works that I do and, in fact, will do greater works than these, because I am going to the Father. (John 14:12)

So we are ambassadors for Christ, since God is making his appeal through us; we entreat you on behalf of Christ, be reconciled to God. (2 Corinthians 5:20)

Holy Heart of Jesus, preserve and strengthen us, especially your priests!

Chapter Twenty-Two

A Promise for Promoters

Those who shall promote this devotion shall have their
names written in my Heart.

W hat does it mean to be written in his Heart? It seems almost too
amazing to contemplate! Scripture tells us:

Can a woman forget her nursing child,
or show no compassion for the child of her womb?
Even these may forget,
yet I will not forget you.
See, I have inscribed you on the palms of my hands. (Isaiah
49:15–16)

St. Margaret Mary wrote,

My divine Master showed me the names of several persons
written in letters of gold on His Sacred Heart, names which
He will never allow to be effaced. These are the names of the
persons who have labored the most to make His Sacred Heart
known and loved.[1]

This seems to indicate that we will know a prominent and perma-
nent place in Jesus's heart if we share the Sacred Heart devotion with
others. I can't think of a better place to be!

Jesus conveyed ten specific Promises to those who devote themselves and their whole hearts to establishing the reign of his Sacred
Heart:

- friendship and divine closeness with him
- great recompenses or special rewards to convey his gratitude
- protection and assistance from the Blessed Virgin Mary and the saints, especially from St. Margaret Mary
- rapid progress in virtue
- the grace of the pure love of God
- special blessings on one's native land and in one's family
- the art of touching the hardest hearts and success in conversions
- strength and consolation in times of trial
- final perseverance and a holy death
- the consolation of possessing his heart[2]

Promoting the devotion to the Sacred Heart of Jesus is a natural extension of the devotion itself. A desire burns in the hearts of those who know his heart. It is a desire to share what they know and experience.

Healing Stories

Carol shares her story:

> When I was fourteen, I received a laminated, pocket-size, oval "badge" of the Sacred Heart in the mail from the Sacred Heart Auto League. I remember thinking that this was odd, since I was too young to drive. The badge had the Sacred Heart on one side and the image of Our Lord pointing to his Sacred Heart on the other. The words surrounding the Sacred Heart read, "Cease, the Heart of Jesus is with me," and, "Sacred Heart of Jesus, thy kingdom come."
>
> Somehow the badge stayed with me through high school, college, and my working years. It even survived one accidental run through the washing machine. I was mortified, and I applied the first (of several) layers of clear packing tape over it, to keep it intact.

I have always been interested in the lives of the saints, and I came across the story of St. Margaret Mary Alacoque, which I found very moving. I studied the picture of Our Lord's appearance to her and read the twelve promises of his Sacred Heart. I remember thinking, "Wow! That would really be something to have my name written in his Heart, 'never to be blotted out,'" and then thinking, "Like that'll ever happen, knowing me."

In 1997, I signed up to be a "guardian" of the Eucharist at a nearby perpetual Adoration chapel. Saturday night, 11 PM to midnight, became my assigned hour. Through the grace of God, I have been going nearly eighteen years now. Often while meditating during Adoration, I have contemplated Jesus's passion. I came to recognize his heart as the source and summit, the treasure house of all God's love. I don't know how to say it except, "It doesn't get any better than this!" You can't ask for anything more. And, oh, how that treasure chest was opened wide: by a soldier's lance.

In May 2011, I was abruptly forced to retire from my job of eighteen and a half years due to a medical condition. Suddenly, I had the terrifying sense of falling down the rabbit hole—A precipitous free-fall, into the dark, and who knows how deep?

Not having to be on the job at 7 AM anymore, I started going to daily Mass. At the same time, I prayed for the Lord to guide me. And he did. I came to be part of a lively and loving, intimate faith community—usually the same people, who sit in the same places every morning. How many times I have recalled with grateful heart the words of a popular hymn, based on Psalm 16: "You give marvelous comrades to me."[3]

I celebrated the Enthronement of the Sacred Heart in my home on October 1, 2015, the feast of St. Thérèse of Lisieux. The holy image I used was one that has been in my family seemingly from "time immemorial." I hung it on the wall in my bedroom, above an altar I made by draping a desk with gold and white linens.

The Sacred Heart has become a focal point of prayer for me. It is a place of peace and sacred space for quiet meditation or perhaps devotional reading. I have made a point of leaving whatever else I'm doing in the house to sit with him for the 3:00 PM Hour of Mercy and recite the Chaplet of Divine Mercy and the Rosary. Sometimes I just look at the tender image of Jesus and, without any effort, just share my thoughts with him, talking out loud.

The notion of being an ambassador for his heart has evolved, such that I now strive to see with his eyes, listen with his ears, and yes, love with his heart.

I search out little ways here and there, now and then, to spread devotion to his Sacred Heart, because I would love to find my name written there one day.

Jesus will love that too!

* * *

I met Melissa during my whirlwind inauguration into the Sacred Heart Apostolate. I was participating in promotion of the Sacred Heart at the World Meeting of Families during the summer of 2015 in Philadelphia. The Sacred Heart Apostolate had a tiny booth in the grand hall with hundreds of other exhibitors. We placed in our booth a beautiful icon of the Sacred Heart. It was our intention to create what we called an "Oasis of Grace" for pilgrims, inviting them to come and rest with the Sacred Heart of Jesus in the midst of all the fanfare.

I was drawn to Melissa's quiet spirit and genuine smile. She seemed to radiate joy, and I wanted to know her story. I found out that her life wasn't perfect, that she had experienced the deepest sorrow that anyone can endure, the loss of a child. Still, she conveyed such hope and love for the Sacred Heart, and her witness was so powerful, that I was deeply touched and wanted to share her work with you.

Melissa knew about the Sacred Heart through her affiliation with the Legion of Mary. She attended a Sacred Heart Mission and felt that the Lord was calling her to the work of promotion. Naturally shy, she sought signs from the Lord that it was truly his desire, and he gave her many confirmations.

The area that Melissa currently focuses on is the promotion of the Sacred Heart in seminaries, a vital and needed ministry. She arranges for each seminarian to receive an image of the Sacred Heart, a Sacred Heart badge, and a book. She also prepares special kits for priest candidates, so that they have everything they need to conduct enthronements and make the Sacred Heart devotion central to their priesthood. For these beautiful and humble efforts, the Lord has rewarded Melissa richly.

First of all, she receives the great benefit of being in contact with many young seminarians and priests who are on fire with the love of the Sacred Heart of Jesus. She also confirms that the Lord showers her with many blessings and that she is filled with a sense of peace when she gazes upon his image. "Sometimes I just rest my head upon him, and he gives me so much confidence!"

I can certainly attest, after meeting and getting to know Melissa, that she is close enough to Jesus to be written on his heart.

* * *

Randy assists Melissa in promoting the Sacred Heart at Notre Dame Seminary in New Orleans, Louisiana. He is a seminarian, a self-described late vocation, having entered at the age of forty-eight.

Randy was introduced to the Sacred Heart devotion when he participated in a Cursillo weekend in 1999. *Cursillo* is a Spanish word that means "short course." The Cursillo is a three-day walk with Christ to learn about the faith. According to Randy, it presents a methodology of how to live the Christian life in union with Christ.

Cursillo participants are encouraged to pray for and accept an apostolate. For Randy, that was helping the Spanish community in his area. He learned the language and immersed himself in outreach and pastoral care. Through this work, he was in contact with devotion to the Sacred Heart, as many Spanish families embrace it. He also developed a deep devotion to Our Lady of Guadalupe.

When he entered seminary in 2013, Randy was approached by an outgoing seminarian who had a dilemma. Soon to be ordained, he needed someone to take his place as coordinator within the seminary, to work with Melissa in the Sacred Heart Apostolate. Without hesitation, Randy volunteered. He helps Melissa distribute the materials and kits for incoming students and returning seminarians and also fields questions. The work of promoting the Sacred Heart, which is not really work at all, both enriches and complements his work with the Spanish apostolate.

One day, Randy was pondering the two central devotions of his heart: Our Lady of Guadalupe and the Sacred Heart. He wondered, "What is the connection?" He asked Jesus and the Blessed Mother in prayer for an answer. Shortly after that, while studying, Randy came across information about a Spanish priest who was preparing to deliver a homily to the indigenous peoples of Mexico about the Catholic faith and Our Lady. Instead, the priest received a lesson from the Indian men: "Our forefathers sacrificed many lives to false gods. Our Lady wants us to sacrifice our lives instead, for love of her son. She wants us to place our hearts into her hands, so that she can bring them to the heart of Jesus."

Randy had his answer! This beautiful explanation has continued to inspire his efforts to promote the Sacred Heart devotion and enthronements.

A friend in a nearby parish wanted to have his home enthroned to the Sacred Heart, but conflicts in scheduling kept getting in the way. Finally, Randy insisted, "Let's get this done!" and he solicited the help of a spiritual brother and the parish priest. When the priest saw the enthronement materials and then experienced the ceremony firsthand, he got very excited. Now he wants to bring enthronements and the devotion to his parish, so that other families can "catch the fire of the Sacred Heart."

For Randy, promoting the Sacred Heart will play a tremendous role in his priesthood. Noting that many of the thirty-five seminarians will go back to serve in dioceses where Catholics are in the minority, he feels strongly that the Sacred Heart is a much-needed source of strength for families and parishes. For if we have the Sacred Heart in the center of what we do, we can never stray.

♥ *Heart Note* ♥

Not all of us can join an apostolate, but we can spread the love of Jesus in our homes, our workplaces, and our parishes. How can you promote devotion to Jesus's Sacred Heart?

PROMISE ELEVEN IN SCRIPTURE

Rejoice that your names are written in heaven. (Luke 10:20)

And this is what he has promised us, eternal life. (1 John 2:25)

Set me as a seal upon your heart,
   as a seal upon your arm;
   for love is strong as death,
   passion fierce as the grave. (Song of Songs 8:6)

Sacred Heart of Jesus, save us all.

Chapter Twenty-Three

A Promise of Divine Grace

I promise you in the excessive mercy of my Heart that my
all-powerful love will grant to all those who receive Holy
Communion on the First Fridays in nine consecutive
months the grace of final perseverance; they shall not die
in my disgrace, nor without receiving their sacraments. My
divine Heart shall be their safe refuge in this last moment.

First Friday devotions are a way to stay connected to the promises of Jesus and remain open to the graces that flow from his heart.
The devotions are the "resuscitation" that keeps our hearts alive and
expectant, hopeful and pure. They strengthen us throughout our lives
and comfort us at the time of our death.

We enter into these devotions not just for ourselves but also for
the sake of others, and for Jesus as well. Jesus asks us to make up for
the ways in which he is neglected by those he loves. While the world
swirls in activity, taking for granted the great mystery of Jesus's presence in it, our First Friday devotions are a way to stop and "make a
statement." We testify to the power of the love of Jesus and show him
our devotion, appreciation, and desire for his heart.

As part of the First Friday devotion, we make reparation for the
persistent wound in the heart of Jesus. In particular, we offer our
First Friday Mass for those in most need of God's love and mercy,
including the souls in Purgatory. In turn, Jesus promises to be with us
in our greatest hour of need, at the time of our death.

HEALING STORIES

Kathleen and her family are a living testament to this promise. She and her husband enthroned their home to the Sacred Heart, and each First Friday they gathered around the image and shared a family time. The main prayer in Kathleen's heart was that her growing family would stay united. Never could she have known how that prayer would be tested. Then, shortly after her twelfth child was born, her husband became seriously ill.

Kathleen cared for her husband at home, along with her twelve children, and the family continued their devotions to the Sacred Heart. "The Sacred Heart was my answer through that last year of my husband's life," Kathleen explained. And as difficult as it became, Kathleen felt tremendous peace. She recalls that when priests would come to their home, they would remark about how peaceful it was. The children remained close through the sickness and ultimate death of their father.

That was thirty years ago, and her grown children and their children remain a united group. They still observe the First Fridays, and Kathleen continues to realize and proclaim that peace is the greatest gift of their devotion to the Sacred Heart.

* * *

Many who practice First Friday devotions have discovered that Jesus doesn't wait for death to fulfill his promise. There can be dead ends in our lives through which Jesus leads us to the joy of his heart. Here's Dawn's story:

> I was twenty-nine years old, and all of my friends were married and starting their families. The one thing I wanted was to get married and be a stay-at-home mom. Still living with my parents, I felt like an overgrown plant sitting in the same small pot where I had been seeded.

I worked in a lab doing research, which didn't involve much socialization, and my biological clock was ticking away. Questions swirled in my mind: *What had I done wrong? Am I supposed to remain unmarried for the rest of my life?*

One Friday evening after work, I roamed the New York City streets alone, until I came upon a Catholic Church. It looked warm and inviting, and there was some kind of function about to take place. I stepped in, and people were praying and preparing for Mass. I asked someone what the occasion was, and he replied, "First Friday Devotions."

I was handed a pamphlet containing the devotions and a few prayers. I read through the pamphlet and was struck by the promises given by Jesus for those who practiced the devotions. Having been raised Catholic, I knew about novenas. I decided to answer the request of Jesus to observe the First Nine Fridays Devotion in honor of his Sacred Heart.

My request was for help in finding a husband. If being married and having kids was not God's will, then God needed to directly tell me what he wanted me to do for the rest of my life, because at that point, everything seemed pointless.

On that first Friday of the month of June, I followed all the things Jesus asked for—reception of Communion in Mass and confession. I would return for the next eight first Fridays to do the same. I felt confident that something would break through: some insight, a new path in life. Most of all, I felt the presence and love of my Lord within me and beside me.

Fairly soon after that, I arranged for a Mass to be said for my father for Father's Day. The church receptionist, Maria, started a conversation about not having a boyfriend and how hard it was to meet anyone decent. I laughed, agreeing with her. But she was still young, I said, while I was running out of time to have kids. Never having met me before, Maria was kind to invite me to go out with her sometime. We exchanged phone numbers, but I never expected the night out would happen.

The First Friday of July was the Fourth of July. I made sure I followed the directives of Jesus for the devotion. Later that evening, I sat alone in my sister's home watching the fireworks, as the rest of the family enjoyed the festivities outside. I felt my life was doomed, and I would spend the rest of my life alone. Again, I reflected on how all of my friends were married, and I was running out of hope.

To my surprise, Maria called the next morning to plan our evening out that night. I agreed but felt a bit silly, since she was twenty-one years old, and I felt like quite an "old lady" at twenty-nine. Maria said she would pick me up at 11 PM! I felt tired and just wanted to go to bed, but it was either go out that night or sit in my doldrums. I hoped that this was part of God's plan.

After arriving at our first destination, Maria decided it was not the place to go. She suggested that we go to another place, where there would be a slightly older crowd. At our second destination, we sat down at a small table and ordered a drink. We noticed two guys in trench coats who appeared to be somewhat out of place. My first impression was that they must have been undercover policemen, but Maria accurately pointed out they were in the military. Their haircuts were the giveaway.

The two men were standing awkwardly, holding their plates in their hands, with no place to sit down. I felt it was my "patriotic duty" and a way to thank them for their service to invite them to join us at our table. We conversed, and eventually, having been a dance major in college, I couldn't resist asking one of the marines to dance. The one I asked had an injury and couldn't, but the other marine took me up on the offer, and we enjoyed a full night of dancing. We four had exchanged names but nothing more. The night ended, the two marines left, and Maria and I returned to our car. My thought was that a relationship with this guy just wasn't part of God's plan.

During the next two weeks, I received word that my grandmother had passed away. When I returned home from her funeral, my mother handed me a phone number, saying a "Mr. Majestic" had called. I laughed, "Mom it's a prank phone call." She insisted it was not, and I pacified her with what I thought would be a useless return call. To my surprise, "Mr. Majestic" was the marine with whom I had danced. He had found my number through a listing, and was asking me out on a date! It was August, the third First Friday of the Sacred Heart Devotion.

On our first date, I realized the great "coincidence" of starting the First Fridays devotion and meeting this marine. We discovered that we had both recently attended a funeral of a grandparent, and I imagined our grandparents meeting in the line at the entrance of heaven, discussing the match of this marine and myself. We continued to date, and I learned that we shared a love for the Bible and that he was a newly confirmed Catholic. It was on our second or third date that he told me that I was the one he was going to marry. I didn't believe him at first, but as time went by and our relationship grew in closeness, I pondered the graces that I was receiving during the nine-month devotion.

I completed the First Friday devotion, telling Jesus thank you so much for placing this person in my life, who was sincere, kind, and spiritually directed. One month later, that kind marine proposed to me.

It was not until much later that I shared with this new Catholic, my fiancé, that I had practiced the Nine First Fridays Devotion in search of a husband. The timing of it all was too coincidental to believe it was not a "God incident." God answered my prayers in a most generous way! Today, I have two beautiful girls and a marriage I know was prepared by God.

Sacred Heart of Jesus, you are most loving and kind, and I am grateful for all the ways you help mankind. Thank you for your promises and your ways of comforting hearts. May this story inspire anyone who feels all is lost, because all is never lost. Within the most Sacred Heart of Jesus, new life comes, and God directly speaks to humanity, his most treasured creation.

♥ *Heart Note* ♥

Explore the ways in which the First Friday devotion is observed in your diocese. How can you participate?

PROMISE TWELVE IN SCRIPTURE

God is not a human being, that he should lie,
or a mortal, that he should change his mind.
Has he promised, and will he not do it?
Has he spoken, and will he not fulfill it? (Numbers 23:19)

The LORD is near to all who call on him,
to all who call on him in truth. (Psalm 145:18)

The one who endures to the end will be saved. (Matthew 24:13)

The one who eats this bread will live forever. (John 6:58)

Heart of Jesus, we rejoice in your promises!

The Triumph of His Love

Permit me to share one final story with you. It's about a young boy I'll call Sebastian, who was diagnosed with a rare childhood cancer at the age of five. His parents had a strong faith but were not able to attend church very much, because they were occupied with traveling back and forth to another state to get treatment for their son. The family was not familiar with the symbols and images associated with their Catholic faith and didn't really know anything about the Sacred Heart devotion.

Sebastian was an amazing kid. He was courageous and selfless and had a sweet spirit about him that everyone noticed. When he went to the clinic for his treatments, the rooms were often filled with other children, struggling just as he was to combat that almighty foe: cancer. Sebastian was always concerned that there be enough toys for everyone. If there were only a few left in the box, he would not take one.

After Sebastian passed away, his parents went to the rectory to plan the funeral liturgy. They seemed unusually at ease with the parish priest, who had expected these parents to be devastated by the loss of their son at the age of eight. The priest inquired how they were managing so well.

They responded that they knew that their son was in heaven. In the hospital room on the day that he died, Sebastian told his parents that he saw angels in the room. When his parents asked him how many, he started to count, "One, two, three, four, five six," then stopped and said that there were too many to count.

Sebastian saw something else that his parents didn't understand: "I see a man with a heart and a lady with a crown." The parents attributed this sighting to a child's whimsical imagination in his time of need. When they asked him, "A man with a heart?" the little boy put his hands together to form a heart in the middle of his chest. A short while later, Sebastian was gone.

The priest smiled at the two bereaved parents calmly sitting before him. "I think I might know this man—and you do too. Let me tell you about that heart."

* * *

It is my hope that this book has taken you on a sacred journey to the center of the heart of Jesus. My prayer is that you have been swept into the divine love story, in which you play a central part. You must know how loved you truly are and how much you can trust in that love to conquer all.

People are hungry for that kind of love. They are also starved for knowledge of the truth and something they can believe in; they are searching for help and healing and someone they can count on. All of this and more come through the promises of the Sacred Heart of Jesus. I know because, through writing this book, I have been witness to what his heart can do.

I have seen it soothe the anger and hurt of a rejected husband and ease the sorrow of a mother burdened by the mental illness of her son. I've seen that Love console grandparents in their anguish over a troubled grandchild. I've watched a single mother draw strength, patience, and dignity from the well of the heart that loves so much. I've seen that Love enkindle a marriage that was nearly dead and throw a lifeline to someone drowning in a sea of depression. All these souls clung to the heart of Jesus and found a remedy.

His is a heart that thirsts and cries out for some return. It is a wounded heart that knows our struggles, shares our sufferings, and bleeds with mercy for us. It is a heart eternally ablaze with blessings and graces reserved for you.

You. You are the object of his desires, the apple of his eye, the design of his heart. There is nothing that he won't do for you. Trust him and live! Proclaim the promises of the Sacred Heart and the triumph of his love.

Sacred Heart of Jesus, thy kingdom come!

Anne Costa
On the Solemnity of the
Sacred Heart, 2016

Preparing for Your Enthronement of the Sacred Heart

ITEMS NEEDED FOR AN ENTHRONEMENT CEREMONY

- An image of the Sacred Heart of Jesus, suitable to occupy a prominent place in your dwelling. This can be blessed by a priest or deacon prior to the ceremony if one will not be in attendance.
- An image or small statue of the Immaculate Heart of Mary, to accompany but not compete with the Sacred Heart image and to be present during the preparation days.
- Bible for Scripture readings
- Rosary or instruction card for days of preparation
- Votive or electric candle to be placed next to the image
- Enthronement ceremonial booklet
- Certificate

The following preparation and ceremonial material is reproduced with permission from the Sacred Heart Apostolate, Inc., in Syracuse, New York.

TRIDUUM FOR ENTHRONEMENT OF THE SACRED HEART: A THREE-DAY PREPARATION

The Enthronement of the Sacred Heart of Jesus is the social reign of Jesus Christ in our homes, parishes, workplaces, schools, communities, and nations. We consecrate ourselves to Jesus, making a covenant of love with him. Our purpose is to bring forth Jesus Christ as the enthroned King of Kings and Lord of Lords, placing everything under the influence of his Sacred Heart.

We prepare for Jesus by reflecting on his heart and our relationship with him as king, brother, and friend. Accompanied by an image of his mother, we make way for the Lord in our hearts, lives, homes, and places of business.

DAY 1

Reflection: To the Heart of Our King, Jesus of Bethlehem

+ Read Luke 1:26–38; 2:1–20; and Matthew 2:1–12

+ Rosary (Third Joyful Mystery: The Nativity of the Lord)

In the Third Joyful Mystery, Jesus is born! God comes to be with us in the flesh as a tiny, helpless baby, thereby consecrating the human family in his image. How do we receive him, and how do we reflect him in our home and our relationships?

+Let Us Pray

Sacred Heart of Jesus, we salute you, for you are the King of Kings, the ruler of families and nations. But sad to say, in many nations, you have been dethroned and rejected. This is mainly because you were dethroned in many families of which the nations are composed.

Loving Master, we want to make up for this insult to Your Divine Majesty by lovingly enthroning you as King of our (*family or organization*). Like Mary and Joseph, like the shepherds and the three kings, we want to give you a royal welcome, as they did, when they adored you in your humble home in Bethlehem. Like them, we have no royal throne to offer you, but we can and will offer something even more pleasing to you. In our (*home or organization*), your throne will be a living throne: the loyal hearts of the members of this (*home or organization*); your royal crown: our acts of love.

O Mary, queen of our (*home or organization*), by your loving submission to the will of God in all things, obtain for us the grace never to sadden the Heart of our King by willful disobedience of his commandments or those of his Church. May it be said of us what the Gospel says of Jesus, "He was subject to them" [see Luke 2:51]. Good St. Joseph, guardian of our (*family or organization*), help us to make this enthronement the beginning of a new life of love in this (*home or organization*). Through the presence of the Sacred Heart of Jesus in our (*family circle or organization*) and through your powerful intercession, may we receive the grace to know our King more personally, love him more ardently, and thus serve him more faithfully. Amen.

+Daily Prayer

Recite this prayer each day of the preparation.

O Christ Jesus, in union with the entire Christian community, we acknowledge you to be King of the universe; all that has been made is created by you. Exercise over us all your sovereign rights. We hereby renew the promises of our baptism, renouncing Satan and all his works and empty promises, and we promise to lead henceforth a truly Christian life. Divine Heart of Jesus, we offer you our poor actions to obtain acknowledgement by every heart of your sacred kingly power. May the kingdom of your peace be firmly established throughout the earth.

Most Sacred Heart of Jesus, your kingdom come through Mary!

Sacred Heart of Jesus, protect us!

Immaculate Heart of Mary, Queen of Heaven, pray for us!

St. Joseph, friend of the Sacred Heart, pray for us!

St. Michael, first champion of the kingship of Christ, pray for us!

Guardian angels, pray for us!

+Sing or play an appropriate hymn.

DAY 2

Intention: To the Heart of Our Brother, Jesus of Nazareth

+Read Luke 2:40–52

+Rosary (Fifth Joyful Mystery: Mary and Joseph find Jesus in the Temple)

In the fifth joyful mystery, Jesus is found by his parents in the temple, and he obediently returns with them to his home in Nazareth. Through this meditation, we reflect on the ways that we discover Jesus in our midst anew through our relationships with those closest to us.

+Let Us Pray

Dear Jesus, Son of God, when we call you "brother," we speak the truth, for you are indeed just that. John told us so in his Gospel: "But to as many as received him, he gave the power of becoming sons of God" [see John 1:12]. Therefore, we are your adopted brothers and sisters and coheirs of heaven. And since you are a king, we have the privilege of being members of a royal family, as were Mary and Joseph.

How honored we will be to have our Brother King come to dwell in our *(humble home or organization),* in order to share our joys and sorrows! Once you are enthroned in our *(family or organization),* we will understand as never before the meaning of the words, "And the Word was made flesh and dwelt among us" (John 1:14). No longer need we envy Mary and Joseph at Nazareth, for your abiding presence in our *(home or organization)* will make our *(family or organization)* another Nazareth, where we will give proof of our love. We will do this especially by the practice of charity: trying to love each other as you love us and to build a more just world in solidarity with the poor.

O Mary, Queen of Nazareth and Mother of Jesus, obtain for us the grace to appreciate the presence of your divine son enthroned in our *(home or organization)*. Grant us a greater love for Jesus ever present in the Blessed Sacrament, a deeper love for the Holy Sacrifice of the Mass, a more ardent longing to unite ourselves as often as possible with our loving Savior in Holy Communion.

Good St. Joseph, you were privileged to share the joys and sorrows of your foster son at Nazareth. Teach us how to share our everyday joys and sorrows here on earth with our brother Jesus, so that one day our entire *(family or organization)* may join you and Mary in sharing the joys of heaven. There we will see our King and brother face-to-face and with you love adore, thank, and praise him for all eternity. Amen.

+Daily Prayer
Recite the Daily Prayer on page 170.
+Sing or play an appropriate hymn.

DAY 3

Intention: To the Heart of Our Friend, Jesus of Bethany
+Read Luke 10:38–42; John 11:1–35
+Rosary (First Sorrowful Mystery: The Agony in the Garden)

Today we remember how Jesus prepared himself in the Garden of Gethsemane to take on all of our burdens and the just punishments for our sins. May we always be ready to accompany him in his passion and never be ashamed of him, as his true friends who love him and live in the mystery of his Sacred Heart.

+Let Us Pray
"My delight is to be with the children of humankind." These words from the book of Proverbs (see 8:32) were certainly spoken about

you, dear Jesus, who came down to share our exile here below. You delight in being with us because we need you and you are our best friend. You love all without exception: saints and sinners, the rich and the poor, the learned and the uneducated. You love all races, all peoples, but above all you love all families. You proved that love by spending thirty years in your home in Nazareth, and during your public life, many times you accepted invitations to visit families. You even told Zacchaeus the sinner, "Today I must stay at your house" (Luke 19:5, *NABRE*).

But there was one family for whom you had a special love, that of Lazarus, Martha, and Mary. How many times did you stay in that beloved family at Bethany! It was there you found rest and solace after the fatigue of your labors and the insulting attacks of your enemies. At Bethany, you were always received as a royal guest, but also you were treated as a brother and friend.

Dear Jesus, once you are enthroned in our *(home or organization)*, we too want to be your true friends. We want you to feel at home with us. We will try to console you for those who do not love you. We will serve you as did Martha; listen to you as did Mary; and thank you as did Lazarus. We feel confident that you will richly bless our *(family or organization)* and all those who invite you into their lives. And if there are in our *(home or organization)* prodigal sons or daughters, lost sheep, sinners dead to the life of grace, we know that you will say to them as you did to Zacchaeus, "Today salvation has come to this house" (Luke 19:9, *NABRE*). You will be to them a loving Father, a Good Shepherd, a Divine Physician, for you are "the Resurrection and the Life."

O Mary, Mother of our best friend, and St. Joseph our patron, obtain for us the grace to make our *(home or organization)* a true Bethany for the Sacred Heart. May our friendship with Jesus be loving, loyal, and lasting. May our daily living with our King and guest bring about a closer union of hearts, of minds, and of wills, so that our entire (*family or organization*), united with the Heart of Jesus here on earth, may remain united with him and the Father and the Holy Spirit in our true home, heaven, for all eternity! Amen.

+Daily Prayer

Recite the Daily Prayer on page 170.

+Sing or play an appropriate hymn.

Other Preparations

Plan to receive the sacrament of reconciliation and celebrate the Eucharist before or on the day of the enthronement ceremony.

Prepare a place of honor for the Sacred Heart image and a place for the Marian image. Have the images blessed in advance. This place of honor will be your prayer place as you live out your covenant of love. Wall tables or shelves are ideal, allowing room for a Bible, rosaries, candles, flowers, and pictures of loved ones.

Requests of the Sacred Heart to St. Margaret Mary

+ Acknowledge Jesus as your King
+ Place an image of the Sacred Heart in your home
+ Consecrate your heart to the Sacred Heart of Jesus
+ Make reparation to Jesus for indifference and hostility to him
+ Live a life of love and confidence in him
+ Make the Sacred Heart of Jesus better known and loved
+ Increase devotion to the Holy Eucharist
+ Celebrate First Fridays

Interior Dispositions of Devotion to the Sacred Heart

+ Worship of Jesus as the Sacred Heart
+ Belief in the merciful love of Jesus
+ Generous return of love to Jesus

+ Reparation for offenses against Jesus, particularly on First Fridays

+ Special love and reverence for the Blessed Sacrament

Enthronement as a Way of Life

In order to keep the enthronement covenant alive, the following practices are recommended:

+ Celebration of the Eucharist, as often as possible and especially on Sundays

+ Faithful use of the sacrament of reconciliation

+ Scripture reading

+ Spiritual reading

+ Holy Hours in the home and Eucharistic Adoration in church

+ Monthly First Friday and First Saturday celebrations

+ Celebration of solemnities and feasts of the Holy Body and Blood of Christ, Sacred Heart, Immaculate Heart of Mary, and Christ the King

+ Making a difference for Christ in society

Related Feast Days to Celebrate

+ St. Margaret Mary Alacoque, October 16

+ St. Claude de la Colombière, February 15

The Enthronement Ceremony for Families

If a Mass will be celebrated, it is recommended that it be a votive Mass of the Sacred Heart, unless there is an overriding liturgical celebration. A house blessing may follow. Then comes the enthronement ceremony.[1]

INTRODUCTION

Facilitator or Priest: Today is a special day for this family, your relatives, and friends. You have invited the Sacred Heart of Jesus to be King of your family. With this enthronement, along with your own commitment to holiness that includes frequent prayer and the increase of devotion to the Holy Eucharist, you will receive the blessings and promises of the Sacred Heart given to St. Margaret Mary by the Sacred Heart of Jesus

Head of the Family: This is one of the most important gatherings of our lives, since the enthronement brings countless blessings to individuals and families. By the enthronement, we proclaim Jesus as King who rules over us through love. But he is more like a father than a ruler. He becomes our generous provider, our friend, our counselor, our spiritual physician, our constant companion, the unseen guest at every meal.

We certainly want him to be all these things, because each and every one of us needs his help. It is not easy to be good and do good. We can't do it alone, but with Jesus's help, we can.

Select a member of the family to read an appropriate Scripture passage, such as Deuteronomy 7:6–11:

For you are a people holy to the Lord, your God; the Lord, your God, has chosen you from all the peoples on the face of the earth to be a people specially his own. It was not because you are more numerous than all the peoples that the Lord set his heart on you and chose you; for you are really the smallest of all peoples. It was because the Lord loved you and because of his fidelity to the oath he had sworn to your ancestors, that the Lord brought you out with a strong hand and redeemed you from the house of slavery, from the hand of Pharaoh, king of Egypt. Know, then, that the Lord, your God, is God: the faithful God who keeps covenant mercy to the thousandth generation toward those who love him and keep his commandments, but who repays with destruction those who hate him; he does not delay with those who hate him, but makes them pay for it. Therefore carefully observe the commandment, the statutes and the ordinances which I command you today. (Deuteronomy 7: 6–11, *NABRE*)

Reflect on this reading, and share with each other what was said to your individual hearts.

Facilitator or Priest: If the Sacred Heart were speaking to you, he might say:

My people, I am your Lord, and I rule through my Heart! I desire to be enthroned as King and Lord of your hearts and of your family, as your brother and friend. I long to share your everyday life, your joys as well as your sorrows.

My people, whom I love so dearly, "Behold, I stand at the door and knock. If anyone hears my voice and opens the door, I will enter his house and dine with him, and he with me" (Revelation 3:20, *NABRE*).

I am Jesus, your Savior, your liberator. I want to save you and your family from the evil forces working to destroy it, to liberate parents and children from the slavery of sin and the shackles of fear, depression, and worry.

I am ready to release in your home the power of my Spirit, the healer, the Consoler, the Sanctifier, the Teacher. But, my people, I will not force my way into your heart or your home. I want to be invited. I am waiting to hear you say to me:

Family: Come, Lord Jesus! Stay with us; we need you! Be the Lord, the Brother, the Friend of our family! Send us your Holy Spirit and give us new hearts, a new spirit! Say to us as you did to John: "Surely I am coming soon" (Revelation 22:20).

Facilitator or Priest: Yes, my people, my Father loves you, I love you, the Holy Spirit loves you. What have you to fear? My wounded heart is the sign and pledge of our merciful love. This heart is open to receive you!

Blessing of the Image by the Priest or Deacon (If Not Blessed in Advance)

Priest or Deacon: Our help is in the name of the Lord.
All: Who made heaven and earth.
Priest or Deacon: The Lord be with you.
All: And with your spirit.
Priest or Deacon: Let us pray.

Almighty, everlasting God, who approve the painting and sculpturing of the images of your saints, so that as often as we gaze upon them we are reminded to imitate their deeds and sanctity: in your kindness we implore you to bless + and sanctify + this image made in honor and in memory of the most Sacred Heart of your only begotten Son, our Lord Jesus Christ; and grant that whosoever in its presence humbly strives to serve and honor the Sacred Heart of your only begotten Son may obtain, through his merits and intercession, grace in this life and everlasting glory in the world to come.

All: Amen.

The priest or deacon here sprinkles the image with holy water.

PROCESSION AND ENTHRONEMENT

The FATHER (or mother) takes the Sacred Heart image into his (her) hands in preparation for the procession to the place of honor. The MOTHER (or a child) carries the Bible. MEMBERS OF THE FAMILY with candles slowly lead the procession to where the image will be placed. Any hymn that proclaims Jesus as Lord or King may be sung. One such song is "To Jesus Christ Our Sovereign King."

Arriving at the throne, the FAMILY gathers in a semicircle. The FATHER (or mother) says while placing the image of the Sacred Heart in the selected place:

"I now enthrone Jesus as King, Lord, and Friend of our family."

The MOTHER (or child) places the Bible near the Sacred Heart image and says:

"We are nourished by the Body and Blood of Christ and the Word of God."

FAMILY: Jesus, we love you, we praise you! We accept your loving rule over our hearts and our family.

MEMBERS OF THE FAMILY *place the candles on either side of the image.*

All: "God is enthroned as King forever" (see Psalm 29:10). "All that the Lord has said, we will hear and do" (Exodus 24:7, *NABRE*).

Facilitator: As an act of loving faith in all of Jesus's teachings (manifestations of his love), and as an act of atonement for those who reject them or do not practice them, let us say the Apostles' Creed.

All: I believe in God, the Father Almighty, Creator of heaven and earth; and in Jesus Christ, his only Son, our Lord; who was conceived by the Holy Spirit, born of the Virgin Mary, suffered under Pontius Pilate, was crucified, died, and was buried. He descended into hell; the third day he arose again from the dead; he ascended into heaven and sits at the right hand of God, the Father Almighty; from there he shall come to judge the living and the dead. I believe in the Holy Spirit, the Holy Catholic Church, the communion of saints, the forgiveness of sins, the resurrection of the body, and life everlasting. Amen.

Kneeling or standing, facing the enthroned image of the Sacred Heart, the family makes their covenant of love with the Heart of Jesus, our King, Lord, and Friend:

Jesus, we enthrone you as King and proclaim you as Lord and Friend of our family. Yes, Lord, we do want you to rule over our hearts and wills through your loving Heart. Share our everyday life, our joys and sorrows. Be our beloved brother, our intimate friend!

Come, Lord Jesus, come! Our hearts and home are open to you. Stay with us; we need you. Release in our home the power of your Spirit, the Healer, the Consoler. Save our family from the evil forces seeking to destroy us.

Our Father in heaven, take away our stony hearts and give us new hearts: unselfish, generous, and pure hearts filled with love for you! Heal our hurts, bind up our wounds, unite us in love. May our love go beyond our family and inspire us to love those in need as Jesus loves us.

Lord Jesus, to your loving, glorified Heart, your wounded Heart, we dedicate, we consecrate our weak, selfish hearts. We humbly acknowledge that without you we can do nothing, but with your help and your grace we can do all things:

> Even though we walk through the valley of the shadow of death,
>   we will fear no evil, for you are with us;
>   your rod and your staff, they comfort us. (see Psalm 23:4)

Mary, Mother of the Church and our mother, help us to make our family a true reflection of your Church—that is, a community of love, a worshiping, praying family.

Good St. Joseph, head of the Holy Family, watch over us as you watched over Jesus and Mary at Nazareth. Obtain for each of us that same loving trust in Divine Providence that sustained you in all your trials.

May the Lord bless us and keep us! May his face shine upon us and be gracious to us! May he look upon this family with kindness and give us peace! And may Almighty God bless us, the Father, the Son, and the Holy Spirit. Amen.

Praise the Lord, now and forever. Amen.

Facilitator: Let us pray the following prayers for the intentions of the Holy Father and for our families:

All: Our Father …

Hail Mary …

Glory Be …

Facilitator *introduces the general intercessions with the following prayer:*

Lord, Jesus, you told us, "Whatever you ask the Father in my name, he will give it to you." In your name and with great confidence, we pray:

All *will respond, "Lord hear our prayer!" or another appropriate response.*

♥ For the grace of being faithful to this covenant with Jesus and our new way of life in him, we pray to the Lord.

♥ For an increase of personal, generous love for Jesus, we pray to the Lord.

♥ For greater trust in his merciful love, we pray to the Lord.

♥ That the Holy Spirit may always find our hearts responsive to his call, we pray to the Lord.

♥ For a deeper appreciation of the greatest gift of the Heart of Jesus, the Eucharist, through frequent Mass and Communion and especially on First Fridays and First Saturdays, we pray to the Lord.

♥ That we may receive the sacrament of reconciliation more often, in order to increase our love for Jesus and avoid sin, we pray to the Lord.

♥ That Bible reading and rosary recitation become part of our daily spiritual formation, we pray to the Lord.

♥ That the Holy Spirit may heal all our hurts and remove from our hearts anything that is preventing us from giving ourselves lovingly to Jesus and one another, we pray to the Lord.

♥ And for any other intentions that you would like to add at this time.

PRAYER OF THANKSGIVING (LONG FORM)

Family: O divine Heart of Jesus, who said to Zacchaeus, "Today I must abide in your home," we thank you for your great mercy in choosing our family from so many others to receive the gift of your presence and of your love and to make of this home a "domestic church," wherein you will receive love, reparation, and consolation for the ingratitude of men.

Unworthy though we be, we thank you for the honor you have bestowed upon us by coming to preside over our home. Gratefully we adore you, overjoyed to see you sharing with us our work, our family problems, and the joys of the members of this portion of the people of God.

We thank you for dwelling with us. From now on, may this home be for you another Bethany where you will always find yourself among friends.

Stay with us, Lord, for as in Nazareth's lowly home, we too have a tender love for the Virgin Mary, your mother, whom you gave us to be our mother. Dispel from our hearts through your holy presence all sorrow and discouragement.

O most faithful friend, if you had been here in time of sorrow, the consoling balm of your peace would have healed those hidden wounds which are known. Stay with us, for perhaps the darkness of trial is about to come upon us. Stay with us, for the night is coming on! The world strives to envelop us in the shadows of unbelief, but we want to be faithful to you, who alone are the Way, the Truth, and the Life. O divine Jesus, let your words to Zacchaeus be fulfilled in our family, "Today salvation has come to this home."

Yes, dear Lord, take up your abode with us, so that we may live in your presence and grow in your love. You alone are King, and you alone will we serve.

May your triumphant Heart, O Jesus, be forever loved, blessed, and glorified in this home! Most Sacred Heart of Jesus, thy kingdom come! Amen!

Prayer of Thanksgiving (Short Form)

Family: Most Sacred Heart of Jesus, we thank you for choosing our family to receive the gift of your presence and of your love. Help make this home another Bethany, where you will always find yourself among friends. Amen.

Consecration to the Immaculate Heart of Mary

This may be done either during the preparation phase for an enthronement or during the enthronement ritual itself.
Facilitator or Priest: Our Holy Father has urged all families to consecrate themselves to the Immaculate Heart of Mary. Therefore, let this special family honor her with this prayer:

Family: Queen of the Most Holy Rosary and tender Mother of the Church, we consecrate ourselves to you and to your Immaculate Heart, and we recommend to your loving care our family, families in our neighborhoods, and families throughout our country.

Please accept our consecration, dearest Mother, and use this family and all families to accomplish your designs in the world. O Spouse of the Holy Spirit, kindle in our hearts and homes the love of purity, the practice of truly Christian family life, and the courage to witness to our faith, even at the cost of ridicule and suffering.

Make our home a Marian shrine, a Eucharistic shrine, a house of prayer, a Christian fortress, a truly domestic Church, so that through us Jesus may be proclaimed as King and Lord and loved as Friend in many homes in our parish and in our country. Amen.

At this time, the father blesses his wife, and they both then bless the children. Or a single head of a household blesses the children.

CERTIFICATE

Each member of the family signs the Family Covenant Certificate, beginning with the head of the family. Then the priest signs it. Guests may sign along the sides or on the reverse of the certificate if the family so desires. This certificate may be framed and placed near the Lord's "throne" in the home. A closing hymn may be sung.

A free, downloadable version of the certificate may be found on the Franciscan Media website at www.FranciscanMedia.org/SacredHeart, or you may obtain one from Enthronement Catalog on the National Enthronement Center website (www.sscc.org).

CELEBRATION

To celebrate this important event, refreshments may be served.

Devotional Prayers

♥ Daily Offering

O Jesus, through the Immaculate Heart of Mary, I offer you all my prayers, works, joys, and sufferings of this day, for all the intentions of your Sacred Heart, in union with the Holy Sacrifice of the Mass throughout the world, in reparation for my sins, for the intentions of all my relatives and friends, and in particular for the intentions of the Holy Father.

♥ Daily Renewal Prayer for the Family

Dear Sacred Heart of Jesus, we renew our pledge of love and loyalty to you. Keep us always close to your loving heart and to the most pure Heart of your Mother. May we love one another more and more each day, forgiving each other's faults as you forgive our sins. Teach us how to see you in those we meet outside our home. Please help us keep our love for you always strong by frequent Mass and Communion.

Thank you, dear Jesus, King and Friend of our family, for all the blessings of today. Protect us during this night. Help us all to get to heaven! Amen.

Most Sacred Heart of Jesus, thy kingdom come!

Immaculate Heart of Mary, pray for our family!

St. Joseph, friend of the Sacred Heart, pray for us!

Our patron saints and guardian angels, pray for us! Amen.

♥ Daily Covenant Renewal for the Individual

Dear Sacred Heart of Jesus, I renew my pledge of love and loyalty to you. Keep me always close to your loving heart and to the most Immaculate Heart of your mother. May I love others more each day, forgiving others' faults as you forgive me of my sins. Teach me to see you in all of my brothers and sisters, loving them as you love them, especially the poor and oppressed, that I may be instrumental in bringing about justice and peace.

Please help me carry my cross daily out of love for you, and help me strengthen this love by frequent participation in the celebration of the Eucharist. Thank you, dear Jesus, for all the blessings of this day. Protect me and others during this night. Help me to live that I might get to heaven.

Most Sacred Heart of Jesus, thy kingdom come!
Immaculate Heart of Mary, pray for me!
St. Joseph, friend of the Sacred Heart, pray for me!
Patron saint and guardian angel, pray for me! Amen.

♥ Praying the Rosary

Integral to devotion of the Sacred Heart and especially to living out the enthronement of the Sacred Heart in daily life is the recitation of the family rosary before the enthroned image. The rosary remains an important "spiritual weapon" and in concert with devotion to the Sacred Heart can combat much of the evil that plagues families in our modern times. *Practical instructions on praying the Rosary are readily found online and in many Catholic prayer books.*

♥ Litany of the Sacred Heart of Jesus

V. Lord, have mercy on us.
R. *Christ, have mercy on us.*
V. Lord, have mercy on us. Christ, hear us.
R. *Christ, graciously hear us.*
V. God the Father of heaven, *have mercy on us.*
God the Son, Redeemer of the world, *have mercy on us.*
God the Holy Spirit, *have mercy on us.*
Holy Trinity, one God, *have mercy on us.*
Heart of Jesus, Son of the eternal Father, *have mercy on us.*
Heart of Jesus, formed by the Holy Spirit in the Virgin Mother's womb...

Heart of Jesus, substantially united to the Word of God…

Heart of Jesus, of infinite majesty…

Heart of Jesus, holy temple of God…

Heart of Jesus, tabernacle of the Most High,..

Heart of Jesus, house of God and gate of heaven,..

Heart of Jesus, glowing furnace of charity,..

Heart of Jesus, vessel of justice and love,..

Heart of Jesus, full of goodness and love,..

Heart of Jesus, abyss of all virtues,..

Heart of Jesus, most worthy of all praise,..

Heart of Jesus, King and center of all hearts,..

Heart of Jesus, in whom are all the treasures of wisdom and
    knowledge,..

Heart of Jesus, in whom dwells all the fullness of the Godhead,..

Heart of Jesus, in whom the Father was well pleased,..

Heart of Jesus, of whose fullness we have all received,..

Heart of Jesus, desire of the everlasting hills,..

Heart of Jesus, patient and rich in mercy,..

Heart of Jesus, rich to all who call upon you,..

Heart of Jesus, fount of life and holiness,..

Heart of Jesus, propitiation for our offenses,..

Heart of Jesus, overwhelmed with reproaches,..

Heart of Jesus, bruised for our iniquities,..

Heart of Jesus, obedient even unto death,..

Heart of Jesus, pierced with a lance,..

Heart of Jesus, source of all consolation,..

Heart of Jesus, our life and resurrection,..

Heart of Jesus, our peace and reconciliation,..

Heart of Jesus, victim for our sins,..

Heart of Jesus, salvation of those who hope in you,..

Heart of Jesus, hope of those who die in you,..

Heart of Jesus, delight of all saints,..

V. Lamb of God, who takest away the sins of the world,

R. *Spare us, O Lord.*

V. Lamb of God, who takest away the sins of the world,

R. *Graciously hear us, O Lord.*

V. Lamb of God, who takest away the sins of the world,

R. *Have mercy on us.*

V. Jesus, meek and humble of heart,

R. *Make our hearts like unto thine.*

Let us pray.

Almighty and eternal God, look upon the heart of thy most beloved Son and upon the praises and satisfaction which he offers thee in the name of sinners; and to those who implore thy mercy, in thy great goodness, grant forgiveness in the name of the same Jesus Christ, thy Son, who livest and reignest with thee forever and ever. Amen.

♥ Prayer to the Sacred Heart

O most holy Heart of Jesus, fountain of every blessing,

I adore you, I love you and will a lively sorrow for my sins.

I offer you this poor heart of mine.

Make me humble, patient, pure, and wholly obedient to your will.

Grant, good Jesus, that I may live in you and for you.

Protect me in the midst of danger; comfort me in my afflictions;

give me health of body, assistance in my temporal needs,

your blessings on all that I do, and the grace of a holy death.

Within your heart I place my every care.

In every need let me come to you with humble trust saying,

Heart of Jesus, help me. Amen.

♥ Act of Consecration to the Sacred Heart of Jesus

BY ST. MARGARET MARY

O Sacred Heart of Jesus, I give and consecrate to thee my actions and pains, my sufferings and my life, in order that my entire being may be devoted to honor, love, and glorify thy Sacred Heart. It is my sincere determination to be and to do all for thy love. I renounce with all my heart all that may be displeasing to thee.

I choose thee, O Sacred Heart, for the only object of my love, the protector of my life, the pledge of my salvation, the remedy of my weakness and inconstancy, the repairer of my past defects, and my safe asylum at the hour of death. Be then, O Heart of Goodness, my advocate near God the Father, and save me from his just anger.

O Heart of Love, in thee I place all my confidence. I fear much from my own malice and weakness, but I hope all from thy goodness. Destroy in me all that displeases or resists thee. Let thy pure love be so deeply impressed on my heart that I may never forget or be separated from thee.

O Jesus, I implore thee, by thy goodness, to let my name be written in thy Sacred Heart, that living and dying in quality of thy slave, I may find all my glory and happiness in thee. Amen.

♥ Contemporary Prayer of Reparation

Lord Jesus, who loves us so much: We have not loved you as we easily might have, nor served you enough in our neighbor as we could have. We are truly sorry for this unfaithful love and promise to do better in the future. Because you accept everything that we do in God's grace when done in a spirit of love and obedience, for reparation we now offer you and your Heart our every thought, word, deed, and suffering in union with your own sufferings.

Join our reparation to that which you ceaselessly offer to the Father in the Mass and in the silence of the tabernacle. Help us to suffer lovingly and to aid those who suffer. Make your redemptive love fruitful in the hearts of all those who will die today, so that all of us may love you forever in heaven. Amen.[1]

♥ Offering of the Holy Hour

My sweet Jesus, I desire to spend this hour with you, to console you and to make some reparation by the love of my poor heart for the agony you suffered in Gethsemane. In that lone hour, you were forsaken, and the creatures whom you created to love you loved you not. The weight of all our sins pressed on you, and mine as well; and for the sorrow which I caused you then by my sins, I will endeavor to repay you now by my love. Strengthen my love, my Jesus, that it may in some small measure give you consolation.

Sacred Heart of Jesus, strengthened in your agony by an angel, comfort us in our agony. Amen.[2]

♥ Efficacious Novena to the Sacred Heart of Jesus

This nine-day prayer is often said prior to the Feast of the Sacred Heart but can be said anytime. The "Our Father," "Hail, Mary," Glory Be," and "Hail, Holy Queen" are traditional Catholic prayers associated with the Rosary, and may be readily found online or in most Catholic prayer books. There are other versions of the novena; this is the one that St. Margaret Mary offered.

O my Jesus, you have said: "Truly I say to you, ask and you will receive, seek and you will find, knock and it will be opened to you." Behold, I knock, I seek, and ask for the grace of *(name your request).* Our Father... Hail Mary... Glory be to the Father...

♥ Sacred Heart of Jesus, I place all my trust in you.

O my Jesus, you have said: "Truly I say to you, if you ask anything of the Father in my name, he will give it to you." Behold, in your name, I ask the Father for the grace of *(name your request).*

Our Father... Hail Mary... Glory be to the Father...

♥ Sacred Heart of Jesus, I place all my trust in you.

O my Jesus, you have said: "Truly I say to you, heaven and earth will pass away, but my words will not pass away." Encouraged by your infallible words, I now ask for the grace of *(name your request).*

Our Father... Hail Mary... Glory be to the Father...

♥ **Sacred Heart of Jesus, I place all my trust in you.**

O Sacred Heart of Jesus, for whom it is impossible not to have compassion on the afflicted, have pity on us miserable sinners and grant us the grace which we ask of you, through the Sorrowful and Immaculate Heart of Mary, your tender mother and ours.

Say the Hail, Holy Queen and add: "St. Joseph, foster father of Jesus, pray for us."[3]

—St. Margaret Mary Alacoque

♥ **A Prayer to St. Margaret Mary Alacoque**

St. Margaret Mary, permitted by the Sacred Heart of Jesus to become partaker of the divine treasures of the Sacred Heart of Jesus, obtain for us, we beseech you, from that adorable Heart, the graces we need. We ask for them with boundless confidence. May the divine Heart of Jesus be willing to grant them to us through your intercession, so that once again he may, through you, be glorified and loved. Amen.

V. Pray for us, O blessed Margaret,

R. that we may be made worthy of the promises of Christ.

Let us pray.

O Lord Jesus Christ, who wondrously opened the unsearchable riches of your heart to blessed Margaret Mary, the virgin: grant unto us, by her merits and our imitation of her, that we may love you in all things and above all things, and may be worthy to have our everlasting dwelling in the same Sacred Heart, who lives and reigns world without end. Amen.[4]

Prayers for Special Circumstances

♥ **Prayer of Trust to the Sacred Heart (in Times of Stress)**

Holy Heart of Jesus, Sweet Sanctuary of rest,
bring peace to my soul and settle my spirit,
especially in the matter of_____.
I vow to place all of my worries and fears
into the wound of your Sacred Heart,
there to be tended to in accordance with your perfect will,
which desires only the best and highest good.
Your love alone is enough, and I surrender to it;
clinging to the hope of a swift resolution
and trusting with confidence in all of your promises. Amen.

♥ **Prayer to the Sacred Heart in Times of Loss or Betrayal**

Sweet Jesus, your heart beats for the brokenhearted,
and you know their pain.
You experienced loss when your friend Lazarus died,
and betrayal when your friends abandoned and rejected you in
your darkest hours.

I ask you for relief and release right now in this time of grief.
I cry out to your heart, seeking comfort and consolation.
Take this present heartache and unite it to your own for the good
of others,
especially _____.
Ease my sorrow,

and fill my heart with hope and light to face another day. Amen.

♥ Prayer to the Sacred Heart for Help to Forgive

Lord Jesus,

my heart feels like an impenetrable stone as I am struggling to
forgive_____.

Please trade my hardened heart for one that flows with mercy like
your own.

Give me the grace to let go of bitterness, a desire for revenge,
and the need for an apology.

Set me free from the captivity of my unforgiving heart
and fill me with your healing love. Amen.

♥ Prayer to the Sacred Heart for Someone Who Is Addicted

Lord, my heart is filled with concern for_____, who is
addicted.

You know and see the disorder and chaos that the addiction is
causing,

and your heart grieves over the distortion of personality and danger
to the soul that results when someone is in the throes of addiction.

I pray that you will please give me the wisdom and spiritual
fortitude

to detach with love and trust in your tender mercies
and that you will give _____ the humility and strength
to seek recovery.

I ask this through the saving grace of your Sacred Heart. Amen.

♥ Prayer to the Sacred Heart When Health Is Failing

Sweet Heart of Jesus,

my health is failing, and I am hurting.

Thank you for my body, which is a great and marvelous gift
and a temple where the Holy Spirit chooses to dwell.

I offer up my current suffering for _____,
accepting whatever you permit to happen to me.
I believe in your healing power and claim your promises of peace,
help in all my afflictions, and the grace of final perseverance.
Help me to resist all fear,
and hide me, Lord, in the haven of your precious heart.
Give me the strength to accept this current state of my health
with joy, holy resignation, and lively hope for the future. Amen.

♥ **Prayer of Thanksgiving and Praise to the Sacred Heart**
Lord, you deserve all honor and praise,
because your love is perfect and your heart sublime.
My heart is filled to overflowing with gratitude
for the many blessings and graces you have bestowed upon me and
    those whom I love.
Forever undeserving, may I always be attentive
and never take for granted the gifts of mercy and love
that flow so freely and generously from your Sacred Heart.
Heart of Jesus, I adore you.
Heart of Jesus, I praise you.
Heart of Jesus, I thank you.
Heart of Jesus, I love you forever and always. Amen.

ENTHRONEMENT MINISTRIES

The National Enthronement Center

P.O. Box 111

Fairhaven, MA 02719-0111

Phone (508) 999-2680

Fax (508) 993-8233

Email necenter@juno.com

The center supplies everything needed for ceremonials.

Sacred Heart Apostolate, Inc.

105 Stanton Ave.

Solvay, NY 13209

Phone (315) 492-6308 or 1 (800) 851-5320

Email sacredhc@verizon.net

www.sacredheartapostolate.com

This is a global movement for creating a civilization of love through enthronement of the Sacred Heart, to renew societies by centering families on the love of God incarnated in the Heart of Christ.

The Sacred Heart Enthronement Network

Phone (614) 798-1792

www.enthronements.com

A complete online resource for do-it-yourself enthronements, devotions, and information on becoming a volunteer missionary or starting a Sacred Heart Enthronement chapter.

Men of the Sacred Hearts of Jesus and Mary

6200 Chicago Rd.

Warren, MI 48092

David Tay, executive director, dtay@menofthesacredhearts.org

MSH@menofthesacredhearts.com

menofthesacredhearts.com

Chapters throughout the United States and Canada can assist you in enthroning the Sacred Heart of Jesus.

Men of the Sacred Hearts, Ohio

Men of the Sacred Hearts of Jesus and Mary

P.O. Box 531053

Cincinnati, OH 45253

Email: info@menofthesacredheartsohio.com

menofthesacredheartsohio.com

The goal of the Men of the Sacred Hearts, Ohio, is to spread the devotion of the Sacred Heart of Jesus to all mankind, enthroning him in homes, schools, businesses, and parishes.

APOSTOLATES

Apostleship of Prayer

1501 S. Layton Blvd.

Milwaukee, WI 53215

Phone: (414) 486-1152

Email: info@apostleshipofprayer.org

apostleshipofprayer.org

The mission of the Apostleship of Prayer is to encourage Christians to make a daily offering of themselves to the Lord for the coming of God's kingdom and the Holy Father's monthly intentions. Nourishing this spiritual program is the love of the Sacred Heart of Jesus.

League of Tarcisius (Tarcisians) of the Sacred Heart

sacredheartholyhour@gmail.com

The purpose of the league is to form boys and girls into apostles of the Sacred Heart, especially by promoting enthronement of the

Sacred Heart. All information about the league, how to form a group, conduct a meeting, and so on is at the website, sacredheartholyhour. com.

The Guard of Honor of the Sacred Heart of Jesus

Guardofhonor.usa@gmail.com

guardofhonor-usa.org

The main end of the Guard of Honor is to console the wounded heart of Jesus by offering a threefold homage of glory, love, and reparation.

Congregation of the Sacred Hearts of Jesus and Mary

P.O. Box 1365

Kaneohe, HI 96744-1365

Phone: (808) 247-5035

Email: info@sscc.org

sacredhearts-sscc-usa.com

The vowed religious men of the Congregation of the Sacred Hearts commit themselves to contemplate, live, and proclaim the love of God to the world through the Sacred Hearts of Jesus and Mary

OTHER GROUPS OF INTEREST

Marian Fathers of the Immaculate Conception

Eden Hill

Stockbridge, MA 01263

(800) 462-7426

divinemercy.org

The Congregation of Marian Fathers of the Immaculate Conception of the Most Blessed Virgin Mary is a fraternal community of conse- crated life in the Roman Catholic Church. In America, the members of the congregation are perhaps best known for their work promoting the message of Divine Mercy from Stockbridge, Massachusetts. They are also known for their devotion to Mary Immaculate, dedication to praying for the poor souls in purgatory, and active service to the Church.

The Legion of Mary

International Centre
Concilium Legionis Mariae
De Montfort House
Morning Star Ave.
Brunswick St.
Dublin 7, Ireland
Tel: +353-1-872-3153
Fax: +353-1-872-6386
Email: concilium@legion-of-mary.ie
For local contacts, check with your parish or diocesan office.

The Legion of Mary is a lay Catholic organization whose members serve the Church on a voluntary basis in almost every country. The object of the Legion of Mary is the glory of God through the holiness of its members, developed by prayer and active cooperation in Mary's and the Church's work.

The Marian Catechist Apostolate

P.O. Box 637
La Crosse, WI 54602-0637
Phone: (608) 782-0011
Email: internationalOffice@MarianCatechist.com
mariancatechist.com

The heart of the Marian Catechist Apostolate is to fulfill Christ's directive to proclaim the Gospel to all nations, so that in knowing God, all might love him; that in loving him, all might serve him; that in serving him, all souls might be saved.

Alacoque, Margaret Mary. *Thoughts and Sayings of St. Margaret Mary for Every Day of the Year*. Sisters of the Visitation of Partridge Green, trans. Rockford, IL: Tan, 1986.

———. *The Letters of St. Margaret Mary Alacoque, Apostle of the Sacred Heart*. Fr. Clarence A. Herbst, SJ, trans. Charlotte, NC: Tan, 2012.

Claret de la Touche, Mother Louise Margaret. *The Sacred Heart and the Priesthood*. Charlotte, NC: Tan, 2009.

Cooper O'Boyle, Donna-Marie. *The Miraculous Medal: Stories, Prayers and Devotions*. Cincinnati: Servant, 2013.

———. *Our Lady of Fatima: 100 Years of Stories, Prayers, and Devotions*. Cincinnati: Servant, 2017.

Croiset, John, SJ. *The Devotion to the Sacred Heart*. Fr. Patrick O'Connell, BD, trans. Charlotte, NC: Tan. 1988.

Gaitley, Michael E., MIC. *33 Days to Morning Glory*. Stockbridge, MA: Marian, 2013.

———. *Consoling the Heart of Jesus*. Stockbridge, MA: Marian, 2010.

Kerns, Vincent, ed. *The Autobiography of St. Margaret Mary*. London: Darton, Longman & Todd, 1976.

Kowalska, Faustina Maria. *Diary: Divine Mercy in My Soul*. Stockbridge, MA: Marian, 2005.

Kubicki, James, SJ. *A Heart on Fire: Rediscovering Devotion to the Sacred Heart of Jesus*. Notre Dame, IN: Ave Maria, 2012.

Larkin, Francis, SSCC. *Enthronement of the Sacred Heart*. Cleveland: National Sacred Heart Enthronement Center, 1997.

———. *Understanding the Heart*. San Francisco: Ignatius, 1975.

O'Donnell, Timothy T., STD. *Heart of the Redeemer*. San Francisco: Ignatius, 1992.

Philip, Mother M., trans. *The Spiritual Direction of Saint Claude de la Colombière*. San Francisco: Ignatius, 1998.

Pope Pius XII. *Haurietis Aquas*, Encyclical on Devotion to the Sacred Heart. Vatican, May 15, 1956.

Tesoriero, Bart, ed. *Sacred Heart Prayer Book*. Phoenix: Aquinas, 2013.

♥ Notes

FOREWORD

1. St. Margaret Mary Alacoque, *Thoughts and Sayings of St. Margaret Mary for Every Day of the Year*, trans. Sisters of the Visitation of Partridge Green (Rockford, Ill.: Tan, 1986), 47–48.

INTRODUCTION

1. Fr. John Croiset, S.J., *The Devotion to the Sacred Heart*, trans. Fr. Patrick O'Connell, BD (Charlotte, N.C.: Tan, 1988), 59.
2. Fr. Francis Larkin, SSCC, *Understanding the Heart* (San Francisco: Ignatius, 1975), 26.

CHAPTER ONE

1. Alacoque, *Thoughts and Sayings*, 97.
2. Augustine, *Confessions*, trans. Henry Chadwick (Oxford, U.K.: Oxford University Press, 2009), 3.11.19, 50.
3. James Kubicki, SJ, *A Heart on Fire: Rediscovering Devotion to the Sacred Heart of Jesus* (Notre Dame, Ind.: Ave Maria, 2012), 15.
4. Larkin, *Understanding the Heart* (San Francisco: Ignatius, 1975), 82–83.
5. St. Augustine, as quoted in Bart Tesoriero, ed., *Sacred Heart Prayer Book* (Phoenix: Aquinas, 2013), 10.
6. Kubicki, 42.
7. Kubicki, 42.
8. Benedictine Convent of Perpetual Adoration, *Saint Gertrude the Great: Herald of Divine Love* (Rockford, Ill.: Tan, 1983), 27.
9. Croiset, 83–84.
10. St. John Chrysostom, "Blood and Water from His Side—Chrysostom," posted at Crossroads Initiative, www.crossroadsinitiative.com. Original post, February 4, 2016 .
11. St. Augustine, as quoted in Deacon Keith Fournier, "Good Friday: The Church Is Born from the Wounded Side of the Crucified Christ," April 22, 2011, Catholic Online, catholic.org.
12. St. Bonaventure, *Mystical Vine*, as quoted by Joseph Cardinal Ratzinger, *Behold the Pierced One* (San Francisco: Ignatius, 1986), 53.
13. Croiset, 57.
14. Rev. Francis Larkin, SSCC, *Enthronement of the Sacred Heart* (Cleveland: Archangel Crusade of Love, 1997), 28.
15. Timothy T. O'Donnell, STD, *Heart of the Redeemer* (San Francisco: Ignatius, 1992), 87–88.

16. Institute of St. Clement I, Pope and Martyr, *The Eucharistic Miracles of the World* (Bardstown, Ky.: Real Presence Eucharistic Education and Adoration Association, 2009), 122.

CHAPTER TWO

1. Alacoque, *Thoughts and Sayings*, 39.

2. St. Margaret Mary Alacoque, Letter to Mother Greyfié, at Semur, *The Letters of St. Margaret Mary Alacoque: Apostle of the Sacred Heart*, trans. Fr. Clarence A. Herbst, SJ (Charlotte, N.C.: Tan, 2012), 50.

3. St. Margaret Mary Alacoque, as quoted in Servants of the Pierced Hearts of Jesus and Mary, "Saint Margaret Mary Alacoque: Apostle and Messenger of the Love of the Sacred Heart," http://www.piercedhearts.org/theology_heart/life_saints/margaret_mary.htm.

4. Croiset, 3.

5. Alacoque, *Thoughts and Sayings*, 79.

6. Alacoque, *Letters*, viii.

7. St. Margaret Mary Alacoque, as quoted by Servants of the Pierced Hearts of Jesus and Mary, http://www.piercedhearts.org/theology_heart/life_saints/margaret_mary.htm.

8. From letter of St. Francis de Sales to St. Jane Frances de Chantal, June 1, 1611, quoted in "History: The Origins of the Guard of Honor," http://www.guardofhonor-usa.org/history/.

9. St. Margaret Mary Alacoque as quoted by Servants of the Pierced Hearts of Jesus and Mary, http://www.piercedhearts.org/theology_heart/life_saints/margaret_mary.htm.

10. Larkin, *Enthronement of the Sacred Heart*, 11.

11. Edward Pace, "Quietism," in The Catholic Encyclopedia, http://www.newadvent.org/cathen/12608c.htm.

12. Alacoque, *Thoughts and Sayings*, 7.

13. Larkin, *Enthronement of the Sacred Heart*, 11.

14. Vincent Kerns, ed., *The Autobiography of St. Margaret Mary* (London: Darton, Longman & Todd, 1976), 44.

15. Larkin, *Enthronement of the Sacred Heart*, 12.

16. Kerns, 46.

17. Larkin, *Enthronement of the Sacred Heart*, 12.

18. Kerns, 47.

19. Mother M. Philip, trans., *The Spiritual Direction of Saint Claude de la Colombière* (San Francisco: Ignatius, 1998), viii.

20. Larkin, *Enthronement of the Sacred Heart*, 14.

21. Kerns, 77–78.

22. Croiset, 43.
23. Philip, 20.
24. Tesoriero, 16.
25. Larkin, *Enthronement of the Sacred Heart*, 17.

CHAPTER THREE

1. Alacoque, *Thoughts and Sayings*, 18.
2. Croiset, 244–245.
3. Act of Consecration to Jesus, http://www.catholic.org/prayers/prayer.php?p=439.
4. Pope Francis, Address to Ecclesial Movements, Vigil of Pentecost, May 18, 2013.
5. O'Donnell, 179.
6. Alacoque, *Thoughts and Sayings*, 8.
7. Alacoque, *Thoughts and Sayings*.46.
8. Fr. Amedeo Guida, Sacred Heart Prayer given in Sunday homily, June 5, 2016, at Sacred Heart Church, Cicero, New York.

CHAPTER FOUR

1. Croiset, 119.
2. Croiset, 120.
3. Alacoque, *Thoughts and Sayings*, 42.
4. Larkin, *Enthronement of the Sacred Heart*, 41
5. Croiset, 253.
6. "A Prayer to the Sacred Heart for Those in Purgatory," quoted at Catholic Online, http://www.catholic.org/prayers/prayer.php?p=2878.

CHAPTER FIVE

1. Philip, 3, 4.
2. Pope Benedict XVI, Homily at the Closing Mass of World Youth Day, August 21, 2005.
3. Philip, 8, 9.
4. Tesoriero, 86.
5. Tesoriero, 87.
6. O'Donnell, 260.
7. Larkin, *Enthronement of the Sacred Heart*, 32.
8. Mission Statement, 2006, http://www.apostleshipofprayer.org/mission/.
9. Alacoque, *Thoughts and Sayings*, 101.
10. Alacoque, *Thoughts and Sayings*, 101.
11. Pope Benedict XVI, Homily for the Solemnity of the Sacred Heart of Jesus, Opening of the Year for Priests, Friday, June 19, 2009.

12. "Important Points to Remember about the Guard of Honor and Who We Are," point 3, www.guardofhonor-usa.org.

13. Prayer of Offering, http://www.guardofhonor-usa.org/prayer-of-offering/.

14. Croiset, 128.

15. St. Francis de Sales, as quoted in Michael Seagriff, ed. *Pondering Tidbits of Truth* (Canastota, New York: n.p., 2015), vol. 2, 11.

16. The Missionaries of the Blessed Sacrament present information about Adoration sites across the United States at their website, acfp2000.com.

CHAPTER SIX

1. Alacoque, *Thoughts and Sayings*, 95.

2. Collect for the feast of St. Margaret Mary Alacoque, *Roman Missal.*

3. St. Francis de Sales, Prayer to the Sacred Heart, http://www. catholicnewsagency.com/resources/prayers/sacred-heart-of-jesus/ prayer-to-the-sacred-heart-by-saint-francis-de-sales/.

4. O'Donnell, Timothy, S.T.D., Heart of the Redeemer, (San Francisco: Ignatius, 1992), p.97.

5. "Prayer to the Shoulder Wound of Jesus," http://www.thesacredheart.com/ shwound.htm.

6. *Saint Gertrude the Great: Herald of Divine Love*, 30.

7. Croiset, chap. 6, "The Devotion Which the Saints Had to the Sacred Heart of Jesus," posted at http://www.catholictradition.org/Two-Hearts/devotion6. htm.

8. Pope Francis, as quoted in Edward Pentin, "Pope Francis' Consecrating the World to Mary Culminates Fatima Celebration," National Catholic Register, October 15, 2013, http://www.ncregister.com/daily-news/pope-francis-consecrating-the-world-to-mary-culminates-fatima-celebration.

CHAPTER SEVEN

1. Larkin, *Enthronement of the Sacred Heart*, 8.

2. This school, now the College of the Sacred Hearts, is now a part of the Pontifical Catholic University. However, the original school was demolished and had to be rebuilt, along with most of the city, after the earthquake.

3. Cardinal Raymond Leo Burke, *Enthronement of the Sacred Heart of Jesus* (La Crosse, Wis.: Marian Catechist Apostolate, 2010), 7.

4. Larkin, *Enthronement of the Sacred Heart,* 126.

5. "League of the Tarcisians of the Sacred Heart," http://sacredheartholyhour. com/tarcisians.html.

6. Fr. John Hardon, SJ, *Teaching the Devotion to the Sacred Heart*, ed. Thomas Diehl, SJ (Chicago: Loyola University Press, 1963), pt. 1, "Principles and

Methodology," posted at http://www.therealpresence.org/archives/Sacred_
Heart/Sacred_Heart_006.htm.

CHAPTER EIGHT

1. "Feast of the Immaculate Heart of the Blessed Virgin Mary," http://www.
   newmanconnection.com/faith/saint/feast-of-the-immaculate-heart-
   of-the-blessed-virgin-mary.
2. Rev. Matthew R. Mauriello, "Devotion to the Immaculate Heart of Mary,"
   University of Dayton, https://udayton.edu/imri/mary/i/immaculate-heart-
   of-mary-devotion.php.
3. Read *The Miraculous Medal: Stories, Prayers, and Devotions* by Donna-Marie
   Cooper O'Boyle (Cincinnati: Servant, 2013) for more on this devotion.
4. *Jesus Living in Mary: Handbook of the Spirituality of St. Louis de Montfort*
   (Litchfield, Conn.: Montfort,1994), introduction, courtesy of the library of
   www.ewtn.com.

CHAPTER NINE

1. Diary quotations are from St. Maria Faustina Kowalska, *Diary: Divine Mercy
   in My Soul* (Stockbridge, Mass.: Marian, 1987). Numbers refer to paragraphs,
   not pages. This entry is from paragraph 367.
2. Kowalska, *Diary*, 570.
3. Dr. Robert Stackpole, STD, "The Difference Is in the Emphasis: The Sacred
   Heart of Jesus and The Divine Mercy, Part Five," 1, http://thedivinemercy.
   org/news/story.php?NID=2354.
4. Guillermo Arias, SJ, "Notes for a Comparative Study of the Devotions to the
   Sacred Heart of Jesus and to the Divine Mercy," 5, http://www.apostleshipof-
   prayer.net/docs/NOTES-FOR-A-COMPARATIVE-STUDY-%20TO-THE-
   SACRED-H-J-EN.pdf.
5. Kowalska, *Diary*, 1485.
6. Kowalska, *Diary*, 1486

CHAPTER TEN

1. Pope Pius XII, *Haurietis Aquas,* Encyclical on Devotion to the Sacred Heart,
   May 15, 1956, nos. 113, 114, Vatican.va.
2. Carl J. Moell, SJ, ed., *Angelus Meditations on the Litany of the Sacred Heart of
   Jesus: Pope John Paul II* (Huntington, Ind.: Our Sunday Visitor, 1992), 103.
3. Cardinal Raymond Burke, as quoted in Caroline Schermerhorn,
   "Enthronement of the Sacred Heart's Comeback," *National Catholic Register,*
   vol. 78, no.42 (October 20, 2012).
4. Pope Benedict XVI, as translated by Stephanie Schmude, in Fr. James
   Kubicki, SJ, "More on World Youth Day," August 23, 2011, http://www.apos-
   tleshipofprayer.org/offeritup/2011/08/more-on-world-youth-day.html.

5. Pope Francis, Angelus Message, June 9, 2013.

CHAPTER TEN

1. Alacoque, *Letters*, 50.
2. Larkin, *Enthronement of the Sacred Heart*, 36.
3. Larkin, *Enthronement of the Sacred Heart*, 79, emphasis added.
4. O'Donnell, STD, *Heart of the Redeemer*, 139.
5. St. Margaret Mary, quoted in Larkin, *Enthronement of the Sacred Heart*, 17–18, emphasis added.
6. Larkin, *Understanding the Heart*, 53.
7. St. Margaret Mary, quoted in Larkin, *Enthronement of the Sacred Heart*, 37.
8. St. Margaret Mary, quoted in Larkin, *Enthronement of the Sacred Heart*, 29.
9. Thomas D. Williams, *The Sacred Heart for Lent: Daily Meditations* (Cincinnati: Servant, 2011), 14.

CHAPTER TWELVE

1. Margaret Mary Alacoque, *Thoughts and Sayings*, 39.
2. Prayer based on Psalm 95:7–8, in "Prayers for Grace and Guidance," ourcatholicprayers.com.

CHAPTER THIRTEEN

1. Vatican II, *Lumen gentium*, Dogmatic Constitution on the Church, no. 11.
2. St. John Paul II, *Familiaris Consortio*, Apostolic Exhortation on the Role of the Christian Family in the Modern World, November 22, 1981, no. 17, Vatican.va.
3. Alacoque, *Thoughts and Sayings*, 37–38

CHAPTER FOURTEEN

1. Alacoque, *Thoughts and Sayings*, 40, 43.

CHAPTER FIFTEEN

1. Larkin, *Enthronement of the Sacred Heart*, 44

CHAPTER SIXTEEN

1. Alacoque, *Thoughts and Sayings*, 36.

CHAPTER SEVENTEEN

1. Pope Francis, homily at St. Anna in the Vatican, March 17, 2013.
2. Pope Francis, homily of March 13, 2015.
3. Larkin, *Enthronement of the Sacred Heart*, 48.
4. Kowalska, *Diary*, 1074.

CHAPTER EIGHTEEN

1. Alacoque, *Thoughts and Sayings*, 13.

2. Alacoque, *Thoughts and Sayings*, 61.

CHAPTER NINETEEN

1. Claude de la Colombière, quoted in Philip, 35.
2. Claude de la Colombière, quoted in Philip, 61.
3. Alacoque, *Thoughts and Sayings*, 80–81.
4. Alacoque, *Thoughts and Sayings*, 79.
5. Mother Teresa, *Words to Live By* (Notre Dame, Ind.: Ave Maria, 1994), 79.

CHAPTER TWENTY

1. Larkin, *Enthronement of the Sacred Heart*, 53, 54.
2. "The Enthronement and Our Times: A Remedy for Present-Day Evils," http://www.catholictradition.org/Two-Hearts/enthronement-2.htm.
3. Pope Pius XI, *Quas Primas*, Encyclical on the Feast of Christ the King, December 11, 1925, 20, quoting Pope Leo XIII, *Annum Sacrum*, Encyclical on Consecration to the Sacred Heart, May 25, 1899.

CHAPTER TWENTY-ONE

1. Quoting Vatican II, *Presbyterorum Ordinis*, no. 10, and *Optatam Totius*, 10, 20; see Acts 1:8.
2. Pope Benedict XVI, General Audience, June 24, 2009.
3. As quoted in B. Nodet, *Jean-Marie Vianney, Curé d'Ars*, 100.
4. Michael Bollinger, "My Encounter with the Sacred Heart," April 28, 2015, semcasual.org.
5. Mother Louise Margaret Claret de la Touche, *The Sacred Heart and the Priesthood* (Charlotte, N.C.: Tan, 2009), xvi–xvii.
6. Claret, xvii.
7. Claret, xii–xiii.

CHAPTER TWENTY-TWO

1. Larkin, *Enthronement of the Sacred Heart*, 45.
2. Croiset, 249–252.
3. Fr. John Foley, S.F., "For You Are My God," based on Psalm 16 (Chicago: New Dawn, 1970).

APPENDIX ONE

1. Ceremonials are also available for singles, lay vocations, prayer communities, religious communities, organizations, apostolates, parishes, dioceses and archdioceses, rectories, seminaries, chanceries, hospitals, orphanages, schools, dorm rooms, institutes of higher learning, and places of business. Contact Sacred Heart Apostolate, 105 Stanton Ave., Solvay, NY 13209, sacredhc@verizon.net.

APPENDIX THREE
1. "Contemporary Prayer of Reparation," http://www.sacredheartalliance.org. au/contemporary-prayer-of-reparation/.
2. Tesoriero, 82.
3. "Efficacious Novena to the Sacred Heart of Jesus," http://ewtn.com/ Devotionals/heart/sh_novena.htm.
4. Adapted from "Prayer to St. Margaret Mary Alacoque," http://catholicism. about.com/od/prayers/qt/Margaret_Mary.htm.

ABOUT THE AUTHOR

Anne Costa is a wife, mother of one young adult daughter, and grateful "revert" to the Catholic faith. She is the bestselling author of six books, including *Refresh Me, Lord! Meditations to Renew a Women's Spirit* and *Embracing Edith Stein: Wisdom for Women.* Anne has been involved in Catholic radio as a producer and the host of *A Servant's Heart* and *Refresh Me, Lord!*

Anne is a soul-stirring speaker, teacher, and retreat leader, delivering messages of hope and healing with a special focus on the spiritual formation of women and girls. With over thirty years of experience as a social worker and human service administrator, Anne combines her professional experience, personal wisdom, and Catholic truth to address issues such as addiction, boundaries in relationships, coping with trauma, and depression. Her own personal transformation is a testimony to the power of prayer, the sacramental life of the Church, and the love that flows from the Sacred Heart of Jesus through the intercession of Mary.

When not writing, Anne devotes her energy to working with the Sacred Heart Apostolate (sacredheartapostolate.com) and the John Paul II Center for Women (jpiicenterforwomen.com).

Contact Anne for speaking events, missions, or retreats at charismatacoach@gmail.com or cmgbooking.com. To learn more about the author's ministry, visit anne-costa.com.